R Programming for Machine Learning

Building Predictive Models

Peter Simon

1

3

Discover others in the series

**"R Programming for Beginners:
Master the Fundamentals of R, Even with Zero
Coding Experience"**

**"R Programming for Bioinformatics: Analysis of
Genomic and Biological Data"**

**"R Programming for Data Analysis:The Complete
Beginner-to-Expert Guide to Unlocking Insights
from Data"**

**"R Programming for Statistical Analysis:Unlock
the Power of Data-Driven Insights"**

Disclaimer

R Programming for Machine Learning by **Peter Simon** is intended solely for educational and informational purposes. The content of this Book is designed to introduce readers to the fundamentals Machine Learning of R programming and to provide general guidance, examples, and best practices within the context of data analysis and related topics.

Introduction

Welcome to "R Programming for Machine Learning: Building Predictive Models." In the fast-paced realm of data science, mastering machine learning has become a crucial competency for professionals across various sectors. Whether you are a data analyst, researcher, or business executive, the ability to construct predictive models will enable you to make well-informed decisions supported by data-driven insights.

R is a robust programming language and software environment tailored for statistical computing and data analysis. Its extensive array of packages and libraries makes it an excellent choice for both machine learning enthusiasts and practitioners. With R, you can investigate, visualize, and extract insights from your data in ways that conventional tools often fall short of achieving. This book seeks to connect theoretical concepts with practical applications by guiding you through the process of developing predictive models using R.

Throughout this book, we will begin with the basics of R programming and machine learning. Key concepts such as supervised and unsupervised learning, datasets, features, and model evaluation metrics will be introduced. Each chapter will focus on specific machine learning techniques, including regression, classification, clustering, and ensemble methods, illustrating how to implement these algorithms using R. You will learn how to preprocess data, handle missing values, and select the right features for your models. We will also cover advanced topics such as hyperparameter tuning, model optimization, and the interpretability of machine learning models. Practical examples and real-world case studies will provide you with hands-on experience, ensuring you can apply what you learn to your own projects.

As you navigate through this book, you'll find exercises and coding examples that reinforce your understanding and encourage exploration beyond the pages. By the end, you will be well-equipped to tackle data analysis challenges, build robust predictive models, and delve deeper into the world of machine learning.

Whether you are just starting your journey in R programming or looking to enhance your existing skills, this book is structured to cater to learners at all levels. Our objective is not simply to teach you how to use R for machine learning but to instill a deep understanding of the concepts that will allow you to think critically and solve problems efficiently in your own have.

Join us as we embark on this exciting exploration of R programming and machine learning—where the potential for innovation and discovery is boundless. Let's get started!

Chapter 1: Introduction to R for Machine Learning

R, which has its roots in the S programming language, has developed into a comprehensive toolkit for data analysts and statisticians, streamlining a wide range of data analysis activities. Its extensive array of packages, impressive graphical capabilities, and active community contribute to its status as a favored option for numerous data science endeavors, particularly in machine learning.

In recent times, machine learning has surged in popularity, empowering businesses and researchers to uncover significant patterns within large datasets. R's vast libraries offer powerful tools that ease the implementation of machine learning algorithms, enabling users to concentrate on crafting effective models instead of dealing with complex programming challenges.

1.2 The Role of R in Machine Learning

Machine learning is a branch of artificial intelligence characterized by algorithms that learn from data to make predictions or decisions based on the provided input. R's flexibility makes it an ideal choice for various phases of a machine learning workflow, encompassing data preprocessing, exploratory data analysis, model training, and evaluation. R offers a myriad of packages dedicated to machine learning, each tailored to specific tasks. For example:

1. The caret package offers a comprehensive interface for the training, tuning, and evaluation of various machine learning models, simplifying the process for beginners. The randomForest package implements the random forest

algorithm, an ensemble technique recognized for its reliability and effectiveness in both classification and regression tasks.

Known for its speed and performance, xgboost is frequently utilized for gradient boosting, enabling users to develop robust models for structured datasets. mlr3 serves as an advanced framework for machine learning in R, facilitating flexible workflows and accommodating a wide range of algorithms, thus providing a rich platform for experimentation. Furthermore, R's visualization libraries, such as ggplot2, equip practitioners with tools to create meaningful visualizations that enhance the communication of results and deepen the understanding of model behavior.

1.3 Setting Up R for Machine Learning

To effectively utilize R for machine learning, you need to set up your development environment. Follow these steps to get started:

Install R: Download and install R from the Comprehensive R Archive Network (CRAN) website. Follow the instructions for your operating system.

Install RStudio: RStudio is an integrated development environment (IDE) for R that enhances the coding experience by providing a user-friendly interface, tools for package management, and integrated support for version control.

Set Up Necessary Packages: Once R and RStudio are installed, it's critical to install the machine learning packages required for your tasks. You can easily install packages from CRAN using the

`install.packages()` function. For example, to install caret, you would run:

```r
install.packages("caret")
```

Load Packages: After installation, use `library()` to load the packages into your R session. For instance:

```r
library(caret)
```

Familiarize Yourself with R: Before diving into machine learning, ensure you are comfortable with the fundamentals of R programming, including data manipulation with dplyr, data visualization with ggplot2, and handling data frames.

1.4 Understanding the Machine Learning Workflow

The process of building a machine learning model in R typically follows a structured workflow. While variations exist depending on the specific project, the essential steps include:

Data Collection: Gather the data relevant to your problem. This data can originate from various sources, including databases, CSV files, or web scraping.

Data Preprocessing: Clean and prepare the data for analysis. This step often involves handling missing values, normalizing data, converting categorical variables into factors, and encoding string labels.

Exploratory Data Analysis (EDA): Visualize and explore the data to gain insights and identify patterns. EDA can help you understand the relationships within the data and inform subsequent modeling decisions.

Feature Engineering: Create new features or modify existing ones to enhance the model's predictive power. This could involve scaling, encoding, or combining features.

Model Training: Select one or more machine learning algorithms and train the models using the prepared data. R's comprehensive libraries streamline this process.

Model Evaluation: Assess the performance of the trained model using appropriate metrics such as accuracy, precision, recall, or F1-score. This step might also involve cross-validation to ensure the model's reliability.

Model Tuning: Optimize the model parameters to improve performance. This often entails hyperparameter tuning methods such as grid search or random search.

Model Deployment: Once satisfied with the model's performance, deploy it for use in practical applications. In the R ecosystem, this could involve exporting predictions or integrating the model into a production environment.

Monitoring and Updating: Continuously monitor the model's performance in real-world scenarios, making updates as necessary to adapt to changing patterns in the data.

R provides a rich, user-friendly environment for machine learning, combining powerful statistical functions with an array of dedicated packages for model building and evaluation. In this chapter, we explored the fundamental aspects of R for machine learning, laying the groundwork for the practical applications that follow in subsequent chapters.

Understanding the Role of R in Machine Learning

One such tool that has been a staple in the data scientist's arsenal is R. This chapter delves into the significance of R in the context of machine learning, exploring its features, advantages, and practical applications.

The R Programming Language: A Brief Overview

R is an open-source programming language and software environment designed for statistical computing and graphics. Developed in the early 1990s, R has since evolved into a powerful language used by statisticians, data analysts, and researchers worldwide. Its extensive package ecosystem, built on the foundational principles of statistical analysis, makes R particularly well-suited for data manipulation, exploration, and visualization—key components in the machine learning workflow.

Key Features of R

Comprehensive Libraries: R is home to a plethora of packages tailored for machine learning, such as

`caret`, `randomForest`, `gbm`, `nnet`, and `xgboost`. These packages provide pre-built functions that streamline model training, evaluation, and tuning, allowing practitioners to focus on application rather than implementation.

Data Visualization: The ability to visualize data is paramount in understanding underlying patterns and trends. R's visualization packages, including `ggplot2` and `plotly`, provide users with tools to create sophisticated visual representations of their data, aiding in exploratory data analysis (EDA).

Statistical Capabilities: As a language rooted in statistics, R excels in implementing a variety of statistical methods and models. This foundational strength enhances machine learning tasks, allowing for more informed feature selection and model evaluation.

Interactivity and Integration: R can be integrated with other programming languages like Python and C++, facilitating a multi-language ecosystem for machine learning projects. Additionally, tools like R Markdown and Shiny enable the creation of interactive reports and dashboards.

The Role of R in Machine Learning Workflows ### 1. Data Preprocessing

Before applying machine learning algorithms, clean and well-prepared data is essential. R provides various functionalities to handle missing values, outliers, and categorical variables. Functions like `na.omit()`,

`filter()`, and `mutate()` in the `dplyr` package simplify tasks associated with data wrangling, while the

`tidyr` package assists in reshaping data for analysis. ### 2. Exploratory Data Analysis (EDA)

EDA is the process of examining datasets to summarize their main characteristics, often utilizing visual methods. With R's rich set of visualization libraries, users can create plots (histograms, boxplots, scatter plots) that communicate insights and guide feature selection.

`ggplot2`, in particular, allows for layered graphics that capture complex relationships within the data.

3. Model Selection and Tuning

R supports a wide range of machine learning algorithms catering to both regression and classification problems. By leveraging packages like `caret`, users can easily compare multiple models and tune hyperparameters. The `train()` function within this package simplifies cross-validation and helps identify the best-performing model based on user-defined metrics.

4. Model Evaluation

Evaluating the effectiveness of machine learning models is crucial for validating their predictive performance. R provides tools for calculating various metrics—such as accuracy, precision, recall, and F1 score—making it easier for practitioners to assess their models. Visualization tools like ROC curves and confusion matrices help in understanding model performance visually.

5. Deployment and Reporting

Once a model has been validated and refined, the next step involves deployment and communication of results. R facilitates reporting through R Markdown, allowing users to generate elegant reports that combine code, output, and narrative text. Moreover, the Shiny package enables developers to build interactive web applications, offering a platform to share insights and conduct real-time data analysis with end users.

Advantages of Using R in Machine Learning

Community and Support: The extensive R community continuously contributes to the development of packages and provides support through forums such as R-bloggers and Stack Overflow, making finding solutions more accessible.

Reproducibility: R's scripting capabilities and integration with RMarkdown ensure that analyses can be reproduced effortlessly, which is a fundamental principle in research and data science.

Diverse Applications: R's capabilities extend beyond traditional statistics; its use in machine learning, bioinformatics, and data visualization makes it a versatile tool across industries.

Learning Curve: Although it may present a learning curve for those new to programming, R's syntax caters well to users with a statistical background, making it an attractive option for analysts transitioning into data science.

Challenges and Limitations

While R is a powerful tool in machine learning, it is not without its challenges. Large datasets may pose computational limitations, as R processes data in-memory. Additionally, those primarily familiar with other programming languages like Python may find R's syntax less intuitive. Furthermore, while R boasts extensive statistical packages, the ongoing development of machine learning libraries in Python has created a competitive landscape.

R has established itself as an essential programming language in the realm of machine learning. Its robust feature set, combined with extensive libraries and visualization capabilities, empowers data scientists and analysts to uncover valuable insights from complex datasets.

Setting Up Your R Environment for ML Projects

This chapter will guide you through the necessary steps to establish a robust and efficient R environment tailored for machine learning projects.

1. Installing R and RStudio ### 1.1 Downloading R

The first step in setting up your R environment is to download and install R.

Visit the CRAN Website: Go to the Comprehensive R Archive Network (CRAN) at https://cran.r-project.org.

Choose Your Operating System: Select your operating system (Windows, macOS, or Linux).

Follow Installation Instructions: Download the installer and follow the appropriate instructions. ### 1.2 Installing RStudio

RStudio is an Integrated Development Environment (IDE) that enhances the R programming experience. It provides a user-friendly interface and useful features such as syntax highlighting, code completion, and debugging tools.

Visit the RStudio Website: Go to https://www.rstudio.com.

Download RStudio Desktop: Select the version

suitable for your operating system. The free version is suitable for most users.

Install RStudio: Follow the installation instructions provided on the website. ## 2. Configuring RStudio

After installing R and RStudio, configuring your workspace will streamline your machine learning workflow.

2.1 Setting Your Working Directory

Your working directory is the location on your computer where R will look for files to read and where it will save files.

Use the command `setwd("path/to/your/directory")` to set your working directory. Make sure to replace the path with your specific folder.

Alternatively, you can set the working directory through the RStudio interface: `Session` > `Set Working Directory` > `Choose Directory...`.

2.2 Creating Projects

RStudio projects help keep your files organized. Each project can have its own working directory, script files, and related data.

Creating a New Project: Click on the `New Project` button in the RStudio Toolbar.

Select the Project Type: Choose whether you want to create a new directory, use an existing directory, or clone a project from a version control system.

Name Your Project: Provide a meaningful name to easily identify your ML project.

3. Installing Necessary Packages

R's rich package ecosystem is one of its main strengths. For machine learning, several key packages can enhance your capabilities. Below are essential packages and instructions for installation.

3.1 Base Packages

You'll need to start by installing some fundamental packages:

```R
install.packages(c("tidyverse", "caret", "randomForest", "e1071", "xgboost"))
```

tidyverse: A collection of R packages designed for data science.

caret: A package for training and evaluating models.

randomForest: Implements the random forest algorithm.

e1071: Contains functions for SVM and other statistical methods.

xgboost: An efficient and flexible implementation of gradient boosting. ### 3.2 Additional Packages

Depending on your specific project requirements, you might want to explore additional packages:

data.table for high-performance data manipulation.

shiny for building interactive web applications.

ggplot2 for advanced data visualization.

caretEnsemble for combining multiple models. To install additional packages, simply use:

```R
install.packages("packageName")
```

Replace `"packageName"` with the desired package's name. ## 4. Version Control with Git

Integrating version control into your workflow enhances collaboration and keeps track of changes made to your code and data.

4.1 Installing Git

Download Git: Visit https://git-scm.com and download the installer for your operating system.

Follow Installation Instructions: Complete the installation, ensuring that the option to use Git from the command line is enabled.

4.2 Configuring Git in RStudio

Go to `Tools` > `Global Options`, then click on the `Git/SVN` tab.

Specify the path to your Git executable and enable version control for your project. ## 5. Ensuring Reproducibility Reproducibility is a key aspect of data science and machine learning projects. To ensure that your analyses can be replicated, consider these practices:

5.1 Using R Markdown

R Markdown is a powerful way to combine code, output, and narrative text in a single document. Create an

`.Rmd` file by selecting `File` > `New File` > `R Markdown...`. ### 5.2 Documenting Your Code

Regularly comment on your code to enhance clarity and explain your thought process. Adopting a consistent coding style will also improve readability.

5.3 Saving Your Workspace

To preserve your workspace and data, regularly save your workspace image via `save.image()` or configure RStudio to save your workspace when you exit.

Setting up your R environment efficiently sets the foundation for successful machine learning projects. With R and RStudio installed, your workspace configured, essential packages in place, version control integrated, and practices for reproducibility established, you're well-equipped to tackle your ML endeavors.

Chapter 2: R Programming For Machine Learning Fundamentals

In the context of machine learning, R provides powerful tools and libraries that enable users to implement complex algorithms with relative ease, making it an ideal choice for both beginners and experienced practitioners.

In this chapter, we will explore the fundamentals of R programming as it applies to machine learning. We will cover key programming concepts, essential libraries, how to prepare data, and implement basic machine learning algorithms. By the end of this chapter, you will have a solid foundation in using R for machine learning tasks.

Getting Started with R

Installation of R and RStudio

Before diving into programming with R, you'll need to install both R and RStudio, a popular integrated development environment (IDE) that enhances the R programming experience.

Install R: Go to the [CRAN website](https://cran.r-project.org/) and download the version of R suitable for your operating system. Follow the installation instructions provided for your platform.

Install RStudio: RStudio can be downloaded from the [RStudio website](https://www.rstudio.com/products/rstudio/download/). Again, select the version that matches your operating system and install it.

Basic R Syntax

Once you have R and RStudio set up, familiarize yourself with the basic syntax and data structures in R:

Comments: Use `#` for single-line comments.

Variables: Assign values using the `<-` or `=` operators. For example:

```R
x <- 10
y = 20
```

Data Types: R has several data types, including:

Numeric: Real numbers (e.g., `3.14`)

Integer: Whole numbers (e.g., `2L`)

Character: Text data (e.g., `"Hello, World!"`)

Logical: Boolean values (`TRUE` or `FALSE`)

Data Structures: R offers various data structures, including:

Vectors: Ordered collections of elements (e.g., `c(1, 2, 3)`).

Matrices: Two-dimensional arrays (e.g., `matrix(1:9, nrow=3)`).

Data Frames: Tabular data structures similar to spreadsheets (e.g., `data.frame(name=c("Alice", "Bob"), age=c(25, 30))`).

Essential Libraries for Machine Learning in R

The R community has developed numerous packages that facilitate machine learning. A few key packages include:

caret: The caret (Classification And REgression Training) package streamlines the model training process, providing tools for data splitting, pre-processing, feature selection, and model tuning.

```R
install.packages("caret") library(caret)
```

randomForest: This package implements the random forest algorithm for classification and regression tasks.

```R
install.packages("randomForest") library(randomForest)
```

ggplot2: While not directly a machine learning tool, ggplot2 is an essential library for data visualization, allowing you to explore and visualize your data effectively.

```R
install.packages("ggplot2") library(ggplot2)
```

dplyr: This package is useful for data manipulation, providing a set of functions for data wrangling and transformation.

```R
install.packages("dplyr")
library(dplyr)
```

Data Preparation

Before jumping into machine learning algorithms, it's crucial to prepare your data. Data preparation is the process of cleaning and transforming raw data into a suitable format for analysis. Key steps include:

Loading Data

You can read data into R from various formats, including CSV, Excel, or databases. For example, loading a CSV file can be done as follows:

```R
data <- read.csv("path/to/your/data.csv")
```

Data Exploration

Exploratory Data Analysis (EDA) helps understand the data's characteristics and uncover underlying patterns. Use functions like `summary()`, `head()`, `str()`, and `ggplot2` visualizations to explore your dataset.

```R
summary(data)
head(data)
str(data)
```

Data Cleaning

Data cleaning involves handling missing values, removing duplicates, and correcting data types. You can manage missing data in several ways:

25

Removing rows with NA:

```R
data <- na.omit(data)
```

Filling missing values:

Use imputation methods or assign a default value using the `dplyr` package:

```R
library(dplyr)
data <- data %>% mutate(column_name = ifelse(is.na(column_name), mean(column_name, na.rm = TRUE), column_name))
```

Data Transformation

Normalization and scaling are essential to prepare data for certain algorithms, especially when features have different units. You can standardize your data as follows:

```R
data$scaled_column <- scale(data$original_column)
```

Implementing Basic Machine Learning Algorithms

With your data prepared, it's time to implement some basic machine learning algorithms in R. Let's consider a simple classification task using the random forest algorithm.

Example: Random Forest Classifier

Split the Data: Divide your data into training and

testing sets.

```R
set.seed(123) # For reproducibility

training_index                                    <-
createDataPartition(data$target_column, p = 0.8, list =
FALSE) train_data <- data[training_index, ]

test_data <- data[-training_index, ]
```

Train the Model: Use the `randomForest` package to
train the model on your training data.

```R library(randomForest)


rf_model    <-    randomForest(target_column    ~    .,
data=train_data, ntree=100)
```

Make Predictions: Evaluate the model by making
predictions on the test data.

```R
predictions <- predict(rf_model, test_data)
```

Evaluate Model Performance: Use confusion matrix
and accuracy to assess the model's performance.

```R
confusion_matrix   <-   table(test_data$target_column,
predictions) accuracy <- sum(diag(confusion_matrix)) /
sum(confusion_matrix)           print(paste("Accuracy:",
```

```
round(accuracy * 100, 2), "%"))
```
```

```

We covered the fundamental aspects of R programming in the context of machine learning. From installation and basic syntax to essential libraries and data preparation techniques, you now have the foundational skills to begin exploring machine learning with R. In subsequent chapters, we will delve deeper into more advanced algorithms and techniques, enhancing your ability to leverage R for complex machine learning tasks.

R Syntax, Data Types, and Basic Operations

In this chapter, we will explore R's syntax, examine its core data types, and practice basic operations that form the foundation of data manipulation and analysis in R.

1. R Syntax

R syntax is straightforward and designed to facilitate data analysis. Each line of R code typically represents a command or a function call, and the basic structure follows a specific set of rules:

1.1 Comments

Comments in R start with a `#`. Anything written after this symbol on the same line is ignored by R.

```R
# This is a comment
x <- 10  # Assigning 10 to variable x
```

```
```

1.2 Assignment

The assignment operator in R can be either `<-` or `=`.
While both serve the same function, `<-` is traditionally
preferred by R programmers.

```R
y <- 5
z = y + x  # z is now 15
```

1.3 Functions

R is equipped with a rich library of built-in functions. The
syntax for a function call consists of the function name
followed by parentheses containing its arguments.

```R
mean_value <- mean(c(1, 2, 3, 4, 5))  # Calculates the
mean of the numbers
```

1.4 Vectors and Data Structures

Vectors are one of the fundamental data structures in R,
and they can be created using the `c()` function.

```R
numbers <- c(1, 2, 3, 4)
```

2. Data Types

Understanding R's data types is crucial for effective

programming and data analysis. The key data types in R include:

2.1 Numeric

Numeric data types can represent both integers and real numbers (floats).

```R
a <- 12.5  # Numeric
b <- 3 # Also numeric, treated as double
```

2.2 Integer

Integer data types can be explicitly defined by appending an `L` after the number.

```R
c <- 10L  # This is an integer
```

2.3 Character

Character data types represent text strings and must be enclosed in either single or double quotes.

```R
name <- "R Language"
```

2.4 Logical

Logical data types can have only two values: `TRUE` or `FALSE`.

```R
is_active <- TRUE
```

2.5 Factor

Factors are used to represent categorical data. They can have levels associated with them.

```R
category <- factor(c("High", "Medium", "Low", "High"))
```

2.6 Data Frames

Data frames are a key data structure in R, used to store tabular data. Each column can contain different types of data.

```R
data_frame <- data.frame( id = 1:3,
name = c("Alice", "Bob", "Charlie"), age = c(25, 30, 35)
)
```

3. Basic Operations

Once you have a grasp of R's syntax and data types, you can perform a variety of basic operations. Here, we will detail some of the most common operations.

3.1 Arithmetic Operations

You can perform standard arithmetic operations in R.

```R
# Addition sum <- 10 + 5
# Subtraction diff <- 10 - 5
# Multiplication product <- 10 * 5
# Division quotient <- 10 / 5
# Exponentiation squared <- 10^2
```

3.2 Logical Operations

Logical operators in R allow for comparison and logical testing.

```R
# Logical comparisons
is_greater <- 5 > 3   # TRUE
is_equal <- 5 == 5   # TRUE
not_true <- !TRUE  # FALSE
# Logical conjunction
both_true <- TRUE & FALSE              #            FALSE
either_true <- TRUE | FALSE     # TRUE
```

3.3 Functions and Vectorized Operations

R's functions are naturally vectorized, allowing you to apply operations across entire vectors.

```R
vector1 <- c(2, 4, 6)
```

vector2 <- c(1, 3, 5)

result <- vector1 + vector2   # Adds corresponding elements # Output: c(3, 7, 11)
```` ` ` ` ````

3.4 Handling Missing Values

Missing values in R are represented by `NA` (Not Available). Standard functions will usually ignore `NA`, but special handling may be necessary.

```` ` ` `R ````

vec <- c(1, 2, NA, 4)

mean_value <- mean(vec, na.rm = TRUE) # Removes NA before calculating mean
```` ` ` ` ````

We have provided an overview of R's syntax, core data types, and basic operations. By familiarizing yourself with these elements, you lay the groundwork for more advanced statistical analyses and programming techniques in R.

Data Structures in R: Vectors, Lists, Matrices, and Data Frames

One of the fundamental features of R is its variety of data structures that allow users to efficiently organize, manipulate, and analyze data. Understanding the primary data structures in R—vectors, lists, matrices, and data frames—is crucial for any R user. This chapter delves into
````

each of these data structures, their characteristics, and their use cases, providing a solid foundation for effective data analysis in R.

1. Vectors

Vectors are the most basic data structure in R and are essential for most data manipulations. A vector is a one-dimensional array that can hold elements of the same type, such as numbers, characters, or logical values.

Creating Vectors

Vectors can be created using the `c()` function, which stands for "combine." Here are a few examples:

```R
# Numeric vector numeric_vector <- c(1, 2, 3, 4.5)
```

```
# Character vector
```

```
character_vector <- c("apple", "banana", "cherry")
```

```
# Logical vector
```

```
logical_vector <- c(TRUE, FALSE, TRUE)
```

Accessing Vector Elements

Elements in a vector can be accessed using bracket notation. R uses one-based indexing:

```R
# Access the second element
```

```
second_element <- numeric_vector[2] # Returns 2
```

```
# Access multiple elements
```

```R
subset_vector <- character_vector[c(1, 3)] # Returns
"apple" and "cherry"
```

Vector Operations

R supports a variety of operations on vectors, including arithmetic operations, logical comparisons, and more:

```R
# Arithmetic on numeric vectors

sum_vector <- numeric_vector + 5 # Adds 5 to each element


# Logical operations

logical_comparison <- numeric_vector > 2 # Returns a logical vector
```

2. Lists

Lists in R are versatile data structures that can hold an ordered collection of objects of different types and sizes. Unlike vectors, lists can contain elements that are not of the same type—such as vectors, matrices, or even other lists.

Creating Lists

You can create a list using the `list()` function:

```R
my_list <- list(name = "Alice", age = 30, scores = c(90, 80, 85))
```

```
```

Accessing List Elements

Accessing elements in a list can be done through double brackets `[[ ]]`, or single brackets `[ ]` for subsetting:

```R
# Access the 'name' element

name <- my_list$name # Returns "Alice"

# Access the 'scores' vector

scores <- my_list[[3]] # Returns c(90, 80, 85)
```

List Operations

Lists allow a range of operations, including adding and modifying elements:

```R
# Adding an element my_list$city <- "New York"

# Modifying an element my_list$age <- 31
```

3. Matrices

Matrices are two-dimensional data structures that hold elements of the same type. They can be thought of as a collection of vectors stacked on top of one another. Matrices are particularly useful for mathematical operations and linear algebra.

Creating Matrices

To create a matrix, you can use the `matrix()` function,

36

specifying the data and dimensions:

```R
my_matrix <- matrix(1:9, nrow = 3, ncol = 3)
```

Accessing Matrix Elements

You can access elements in a matrix using two indices: one for rows and one for columns:

```R
# Access the element in the 2nd row, 3rd column element <- my_matrix[2, 3] # Returns 6
# Access an entire row
second_row <- my_matrix[2, ] # Returns the second row as a vector
```

Matrix Operations

R offers numerous functions for matrix operations, including addition, multiplication, and transposition:

```R
# Transpose of a matrix transposed_matrix <- t(my_matrix)
# Matrix multiplication
result <- my_matrix %*% transposed_matrix
```

4. Data Frames

Data frames are perhaps the most widely used data structure in R, especially in data analysis. A data frame can be thought of as a table of rows and columns, where each column can contain different types of data.

Creating Data Frames

To create a data frame, you can use the `data.frame()` function:

```R
my_data_frame <- data.frame(
Name = c("Alice", "Bob", "Charlie"), Age = c(30, 25, 35),
Score = c(90, 85, 88)
)
```

Accessing Data Frame Elements

Data frame elements can be accessed using either the `$` operator or bracket notation:

```R
# Access a column
ages <- my_data_frame$Age # Returns a vector of ages
# Access a specific row and column
charlie_score <- my_data_frame[3, "Score"] # Returns 88
```

Data Frame Operations

Data frames come with a variety of functions for filtering, summarizing, and transforming data:

```R
# Filtering data

above_30 <- subset(my_data_frame, Age > 30)

# Adding a new column

my_data_frame$Passed <- my_data_frame$Score > 85
```

Understanding the four fundamental data structures—vectors, lists, matrices, and data frames—is essential for effectively working with data in R. Each data structure has its unique features and use cases, making R a powerful tool for data analysis and statistical modeling.

Chapter 3: Data Manipulation with tidyverse

The tidyverse, a collection of R packages designed for data science, provides a cohesive and user-friendly approach to data manipulation. In this chapter, we will explore the core principles behind data manipulation in R using the tidyverse, focusing on essential packages like `dplyr`, `tidyr`, and `ggplot2` for visual representation of the data.

Introduction to tidyverse

The tidyverse is an ecosystem of packages that share an underlying philosophy and design principles. It emphasizes tidy data, where each variable is in its column, each observation is in its row, and each type of observational unit forms a table. This structure enables users to employ a uniform approach to data manipulation and visualization, allowing for clear and efficient code.

To begin our journey into the tidyverse, let's ensure that we have it properly installed and loaded in our R environment. You can install the tidyverse package from CRAN by running the following command:

```R
install.packages("tidyverse")
```

After installation, load the tidyverse into your session:

```R
library(tidyverse)
```

Now, let's dive into the core components of data manipulation using tidyverse. ## Understanding `dplyr`

The `dplyr` package is arguably the backbone of the tidyverse for data manipulation. It provides a set of functions that enable users to perform common data manipulation tasks such as filtering rows, selecting columns, arranging data, summarizing values, and adding new columns.

Key dplyr Functions

Filter: This function is used to subset rows based on specific conditions.

```R
# Filtering rows where the value in the 'age' column is greater than 30 df_filtered <- df %>% filter(age > 30)
```

Select: Allows users to choose specific columns to keep in the dataset.

```R
# Selecting only the 'name' and 'age' columns df_selected <- df %>% select(name, age)
```

Arrange: This function helps reorder the rows of a dataset.

```R
# Arranging the dataframe by age in ascending order df_arranged <- df %>% arrange(age)
```

Mutate: You can create new columns or modify existing ones using `mutate`.

```R
# Creating a new column 'age_in_months'
df_mutated <- df %>% mutate(age_in_months = age * 12)
```

Summarize and Group By: These functions enable summarization of data by groups.

```R
# Calculating the average age by gender
df_summary <- df %>% group_by(gender) %>% summarize(avg_age = mean(age, na.rm = TRUE))
```

Chaining Commands with Pipes

A key feature of `dplyr` is the use of the pipe operator (`%>%`). It allows users to chain multiple commands together in a readable way, making the code more intuitive and linear.

```R
df_cleaned <- df %>% filter(!is.na(age)) %>% select(name, age) %>% arrange(age)
```

Reshaping Data with `tidyr`

Data often comes in different shapes that may not be conducive to analysis. The `tidyr` package helps users reshape their data with functions tailored to convert between wide and long formats.

Key tidyr Functions

Gather: This function is used to convert data from wide format to long format, ideal for handling multiple measurements per subject.

```R
# Converting wide to long

long_data <- df %>% gather(key = "measurement", value = "value", measurement1:measurementN)
```

Spread: The opposite of gather, this function takes long format data and spreads it into a wider format.

```R
wide_data <- long_data %>% spread(key = measurement, value = value)
```

Separate and Unite: These functions split and combine columns, respectively.

```R
# Separating a column into two

df_separated <- df %>% separate(col = "full_name", into = c("first_name", "last_name"), sep = " ")

# Combining two columns into one

df_united <- df_separated %>% unite("full_name",
```

first_name, last_name, sep = " ")
```

## Visualizing Data with `ggplot2`

While data manipulation is crucial, visualizing your findings elevates your analyses. The `ggplot2` package, also part of the tidyverse, provides a robust visualization framework based on the grammar of graphics.

### Creating Basic Plots

To create a basic plot, you need to start with the `ggplot` function. Here's a simple scatter plot example:

```R
ggplot(data = df, aes(x = age, y = height)) + geom_point()
+
labs(title = "Scatter Plot of Age vs Height", x = "Age (years)", y = "Height (cm)")
```

In `ggplot2`, layers can be added to enhance visualizations:

geom_point() for scatterplots

geom_line() for line graphs

geom_bar() for bar charts

labs() to label titles and axes

We explored the foundational aspects of data manipulation using the tidyverse in R programming. The

`dplyr` package allows for efficient and expressive data manipulation, while `tidyr` facilitates reshaping datasets
```

for analysis. Coupled with `ggplot2`, the tidyverse provides a comprehensive toolkit for data science.

Cleaning and Transforming Data with dplyr

In this chapter, we will explore the main functionalities of `dplyr` for data manipulation and how you can apply them in your data analysis workflow.

Introduction to dplyr

`dplyr` is part of the `tidyverse`, a collection of R packages designed to make data science easier. It provides intuitive functions that make working with data frames simpler and more intuitive. With `dplyr`, you can manipulate data using a consistent set of verbs. The primary verbs we will focus on are:

`select()`: Choose specific columns.

`filter()`: Subset rows based on conditions.

`arrange()`: Reorder rows.

`mutate()`: Create or modify columns.

`summarize()`: Generate summary statistics.

`group_by()`: Group data for aggregation. ### Setting Up dplyr

To start using `dplyr`, you need to install and load the package. You can do so with the following commands:

```R

install.packages("dplyr") # Install dplyr library(dplyr) #
Load dplyr
```

```
```

Now that you have `dplyr` installed and loaded, let's apply it to some example datasets. ## Loading Example Data

As a demonstration, let's work with the built-in `mtcars` dataset, which contains specifications and performance of various car models:

```R data(mtcars)
```

head(mtcars) # Display the first few rows of the dataset
```
```

Selecting Columns with select()

To narrow down the data to only the columns you need, use `select()`. For example, to select the `mpg`, `cyl`, and `hp` columns:

```R
```

selected_data <- mtcars %>% select(mpg, cyl, hp)

head(selected_data)
```
```

Filtering Rows with filter()

To filter rows based on certain conditions, `filter()` is your go-to function. If you want to keep only the cars with more than 20 miles per gallon:

```R
```

filtered_data <- mtcars %>% filter(mpg > 20)

head(filtered_data)

```
```

Arranging Rows with arrange()

To sort the dataset based on one or more columns, you can use `arrange()`. For example, if you want to sort the cars by horsepower in descending order:

```R
arranged_data <- mtcars %>% arrange(desc(hp))
head(arranged_data)
```

Creating or Modifying Columns with mutate()

To add new columns or modify existing ones, `mutate()` is helpful. Let's say we want to calculate the weight-to-horsepower ratio and add it as a new column:

```R
mutated_data <- mtcars %>% mutate(weight_hp_ratio = wt / hp)
head(mutated_data)
```

Generating Summary Statistics with summarize()

When performing data analysis, summarization is essential. Use `summarize()` in combination with

`group_by()` to calculate statistics for different groups. For instance, to calculate the average miles per gallon for each cylinder group:

```R
summary_data <- mtcars %>% group_by(cyl) %>%
```

```R
summarize(avg_mpg = mean(mpg))
print(summary_data)
```

Chaining Operations with the Pipe Operator (%>%)

One of the strengths of `dplyr` is its ability to chain operations together using the pipe operator (`%>%`). This operator makes your code more readable by allowing you to pass the output of one function directly into another. The following example combines several steps into one fluid operation:

```R
cleaned_data <- mtcars %>% filter(mpg > 20) %>%
mutate(weight_hp_ratio = wt / hp) %>% select(mpg, cyl, hp, weight_hp_ratio) %>% arrange(desc(hp))
head(cleaned_data)
```

Handling Missing Values

Data cleaning often involves addressing missing values, which can distort your analysis. To filter out rows with `NA` values, you can use:

```R
cleaned_data <- mtcars %>% filter(!is.na(hp))
head(cleaned_data)
```

Alternatively, if you want to replace missing values with a

specific value, you can use `mutate()`:

```R
mtcars <- mtcars %>%

mutate(hp = ifelse(is.na(hp), mean(hp, na.rm = TRUE),
hp))
```

We explored the powerful data manipulation capabilities of the `dplyr` package in R. From selecting specific columns to filtering, arranging, and creating new data, `dplyr` provides an easy and efficient way to clean and transform datasets. By mastering these operations, you will streamline your data analysis process and derive insights more effectively.

Data Wrangling with tidyr and readr

This chapter will cover the fundamental concepts and common functions of `tidyr` and `readr`, equipping you with the skills to clean and reshape your data effectively.

1. Introduction to data wrangling

Data wrangling refers to the process of acquiring, cleaning, and transforming raw data into a structured format that facilitates analysis. This process is essential because raw data often comes with inconsistencies, missing values, and formats that are not conducive to analysis. The goal of data wrangling is to create a tidy dataset, following the principles of tidy data, where:

Each variable forms a column.

Each observation forms a row.

Each type of observational unit forms a table.

By adhering to these principles, you ensure that your data is straightforward to work with, particularly when using R and its various data analysis tools.

2. Introduction to readr ### 2.1. What is readr?

`readr` is a package in the `tidyverse` that provides a fast and efficient way to read rectangular data such as CSV files, TSV files, and other similar formats. It simplifies the import process and automatically converts data types to their appropriate formats, providing seamless integration with the rest of the tidyverse.

2.2. Key Functions

read_csv(): Reads a comma-separated values file, transforming it into a tibble (a modern take on data frames in R).

```R
library(readr)
data <- read_csv("data/my_data.csv")
```

read_tsv(): Reads a tab-separated values file in a similar fashion to `read_csv()`.

```R
data <- read_tsv("data/my_data.tsv")
```

read_delim(): Reads files with a user-defined

delimiter.

```R
data <- read_delim("data/my_data.txt", delim = ";")
```

write_csv(): Saves a tibble as a CSV file.

```R
write_csv(data, "data/my_data_output.csv")
```

2.3. Handling Missing Values

`readr` also provides options to handle missing values during the import process:

Setting the `na` argument to a character vector will specify additional strings to treat as missing values.

```R
data <- read_csv("data/my_data.csv", na = c("", "NA", "N/A"))
```

3. Introduction to tidyr ### 3.1. What is tidyr?

`tidyr` is another package from the `tidyverse`, designed specifically for tidying and reshaping your data. It provides a comprehensive set of functions to help transform messy data into a tidy format.

3.2. Key Functions

pivot_longer(): Converts data from a wide format to a long format. This is useful for situations where multiple columns represent a single variable.

```R
longer_data <- pivot_longer(data, cols = c("variable1", "variable2"), names_to = "variable", values_to = "value")
```

pivot_wider(): Converts data from a long format to a wide format. This function is useful for summarizing data and creating a more organized structure.

```R
wider_data <- pivot_wider(longer_data, names_from = "variable", values_from = "value")
```

separate(): Splits a single column into multiple columns based on a delimiter.

```R
data <- separate(data, col = "full_name", into = c("first_name", "last_name"), sep = " ")
```

unite(): Combines multiple columns into a single column.

```R
data <- unite(data, col = "full_name", first_name, last_name, sep = " ")
```

```
```

3.3. Dealing with Missing Values

`tidyr` functions also offer flexible handling of missing values. For example:

drop_na(): Removes rows with missing values from selected columns or the entire dataset.

```R
clean_data <- drop_na(data, column_name)
```

fill(): Fills in missing values with the last observation or a specified value.

```R
filled_data <- fill(data, column_name)
```

4. A Practical Example

To see `readr` and `tidyr` in action, let's walk through a practical example that encompasses importing, tidying, and cleaning data.

Example 1: Loading and Tidying Data

Load the data:

Assume we have a CSV file named `sales_data.csv`, which consists of sales transactions. We import it using `read_csv()`.

```R
```

```
sales_data <- read_csv("data/sales_data.csv")
```
` ` `

Inspect the data:

Before we start tidying, it's good practice to inspect the data.

```R
glimpse(sales_data)
```
` ` `

Tidying the data:

Suppose we realize that our `sales_data` is in wide format, where different columns represent sales in different regions. We can pivot it to a long format.

```R
tidy_sales <- pivot_longer(sales_data, cols = starts_with("sales_"), names_to = "region", values_to = "amount")
```
` ` `

Handling missing values:

If there are missing sales amounts for any regions, we want to remove those entries:

```R
tidy_sales <- drop_na(tidy_sales)
```
` ` `

Saving the tidied data:

Finally, we can save the tidied dataset back to a CSV file.

```R
write_csv(tidy_sales, "data/tidy_sales_data.csv")
```

We explored the essential packages `readr` and `tidyr` for data wrangling in R. By incorporating these packages into your data analysis workflow, you can efficiently import, clean, and reshape your data, setting the stage for insightful analysis. Mastery of data wrangling techniques will elevate the quality of your analyses and enhance your overall productivity in R programming.

Chapter 4: Data Visualization for Machine Learning

Data visualization is a crucial step in the machine learning workflow. It helps in understanding the data, identifying patterns, and communicating results effectively. R programming, with a rich ecosystem of packages designed for data visualization, offers powerful tools for this purpose. In this chapter, we will explore various techniques and packages in R for visualizing data in the context of machine learning.

4.1 Importance of Data Visualization in Machine Learning

Before diving into the specifics, it's essential to recognize why data visualization is so important:

Understanding Data Distribution: Visualizations allow practitioners to grasp the underlying distribution of their data. This understanding aids in selecting appropriate models and techniques based on the data characteristics.

Identifying Relationships: Visualizations can uncover relationships between variables, critical for feature engineering and model selection.

Detecting Outliers: Visual techniques can help identify outliers or anomalies in data which can significantly affect the model's performance.

Evaluating Model Performance: Once models are built, visualizations are employed to assess how well these models perform on unseen data.

Communicating Results: Effective visualization

communicates findings to stakeholders in a more accessible manner than raw numbers or tables.

4.2 Popular R Packages for Data Visualization

R has several packages tailored for different visualization needs. Here are some key packages:

ggplot2: A powerful and flexible package based on the grammar of graphics, enabling the creation of complex multi-layered visualizations.

plotly: Provides interactive plots and is great for web applications or presentations.

lattice: An alternative to ggplot2, particularly useful for creating multi-panel plots.

shiny: While primarily a web application framework, it allows for interactive visualizations within user interfaces.

DataExplorer: A package aimed at exploratory data analysis, automating the process of creating various plots.

4.3 Basic Visualization Techniques ### 4.3.1 Univariate Analysis

Histograms and Density Plots:

Use `ggplot2` to create a histogram to visualize the distribution of a numeric variable.

```R
library(ggplot2)

ggplot(data, aes(x = variable)) +

geom_histogram(bins = 30, fill = 'blue', color = 'black') +
labs(title = 'Histogram of Variable', x = 'Variable', y = 'Count')
```

```
```

Boxplots:

Boxplots are ideal for identifying outliers and understanding the spread of the data.

```R
ggplot(data, aes(y = variable)) + geom_boxplot(fill = 'lightblue') +

labs(title = 'Boxplot of Variable', y = 'Value')
```

4.3.2 Bivariate Analysis

Scatter Plots:

They are effective in identifying relationships between two numeric variables.

```R
ggplot(data, aes(x = var1, y = var2)) + geom_point(color = 'red') +

labs(title = 'Scatter Plot of Var1 vs Var2', x = 'Var1', y = 'Var2')
```

Heatmaps:

Useful for visualizing correlations between multiple variables.

```R library(reshape2)
correlation_matrix <- cor(data) melted_cormat <- melt(correlation_matrix)
```

```R
ggplot(melted_cormat, aes(Var1, Var2, fill = value)) +
geom_tile() +

scale_fill_gradient2(low = "blue", high = "red", mid =
"white", midpoint = 0, limit = c(-1,1), space = "Lab",
name="Pearson\nCorrelation") +

theme_minimal() +

labs(title = 'Correlation Heatmap')
```

4.3.3 Multivariate Analysis

Pair Plots:

Allows visualization of pairwise relationships in a dataset.

```R
pairs(data)
```

Principal Component Analysis (PCA):

Visualize the results of PCA to reduce dimensionality and detect clustering.

```R
pca_result <- prcomp(data, scale. = TRUE) pca_data <-
as.data.frame(pca_result$x) ggplot(pca_data, aes(x =
PC1, y = PC2)) +

geom_point() + labs(title = 'PCA Plot')

```

4.4 Leveraging Visualizations in Model Evaluation

After model training, it's essential to evaluate its

performance visually:

Confusion Matrix:

A heatmap can represent the confusion matrix to analyze classification results.

```R
library(caret)
```

```
confusion_matrix <- confusionMatrix(predicted, actual)
confusion_matrix_table                          <-
as.data.frame(confusion_matrix$table)
ggplot(confusion_matrix_table, aes(x = Prediction, y =
Reference)) +

geom_tile(aes(fill    =    Freq),    color    =    'white')    +
scale_fill_gradient(low = "white", high = "blue") +
labs(title = 'Confusion Matrix')
```

ROC Curves:

Plotting the ROC curve aids in assessing the quality of a classification model.

```R
library(pROC)
```

```
roc_object    <-    roc(actual,    predicted_probabilities)
plot(roc_object, col = "blue", lwd = 2)
```

4.5 Interactive Visualizations

With   the   rise   of   web   applications,   interactive visualizations are becoming increasingly popular. The

plotly package enables users to add interactivity to existing `ggplot2` visualizations.

```R
library(plotly)
p <- ggplot(data, aes(x = var1, y = var2)) + geom_point()
ggplotly(p)
```

Data visualization is an integral part of the machine learning process, helping data scientists and analysts make sense of complex datasets and communicate insights. R offers a wide range of visualization tools, from basic plots to advanced interactive charts. By utilizing these resources thoughtfully, practitioners can enhance their understanding of data and improve their model-building efforts.

Exploring Data with ggplot2

Developed by Hadley Wickham, ggplot2 is based on the Grammar of Graphics, which provides a coherent system for describing and building visualizations. In this chapter, we will explore the foundational concepts of ggplot2, create a variety of visualizations, and discuss best practices for data visualization.

1. Getting Started with ggplot2

Before diving into visualizations, we need to ensure that ggplot2 is installed and loaded into our R environment. This can be done using the following commands:

```R
# Install ggplot2 if you haven't already
install.packages("ggplot2")
# Load ggplot2
library(ggplot2)
```

```
```

1.1 Understanding the Grammar of Graphics

At the core of ggplot2 is the concept of the Grammar of Graphics, which allows users to build visualizations layer by layer. This involves specifying:

Data: The dataset to be used for the visualization.

Aesthetics: The visual properties (like size, shape, color) that represent data variables.

Geometries: The type of visualization (such as points, lines, bars) used to represent data.

Statistics: The measurement applied to the data (like mean or count).

Coordinates: The type of axis (like Cartesian or polar) used for plotting.

Facets: The technique of creating small multiples which display the same combination of variables across different panels.

2. Basic Features of ggplot2

Once ggplot2 is installed and loaded, we can start creating our first plot. The basic structure of a ggplot2 command is as follows:

```R

ggplot(data = <your_data>) +

<geometric_function>(aes(x = <x_axis>, y = <y_axis>))
```
```

### 2.1 The `aes()` Function
```

The `aes()` (aesthetic mapping) function is essential for defining how variables in the data are mapped to visual properties. For example:

```R
ggplot(mpg, aes(x = displ, y = hwy)) + geom_point()
```

This example creates a scatter plot of engine displacement (`displ`) against highway miles per gallon (`hwy`) from the `mpg` dataset included in ggplot2.

2.2 Common Geometries

Several geometries can be used in ggplot2, including:

geom_point(): For scatter plots.

geom_line(): For line plots.

geom_bar(): For bar charts.

geom_histogram(): For histograms.

geom_boxplot(): For box plots. ## 3. Customizing Plots

One of the strengths of ggplot2 is its ability to customize visualizations to suit specific needs. ### 3.1 Adding Titles and Labels

You can enhance your plots by adding titles and labels using `labs()`:

```R
ggplot(mpg, aes(x = displ, y = hwy)) + geom_point() +
labs(title = "Engine Displacement vs. Highway MPG", x =
```

"Engine Displacement (liters)",

y = "Highway MPG")

```
```

3.2 Changing Themes

ggplot2 offers several built-in themes to change the overall appearance of the plots. For instance:

```R
ggplot(mpg, aes(x = displ, y = hwy)) + geom_point() +
theme_minimal()
```

3.3 Color and Size Aesthetics

You can add color, size, and shape aesthetics to visualizations to convey additional information:

```R
ggplot(mpg, aes(x = displ, y = hwy, color = class, size = year)) + geom_point() +
labs(title = "Engine Displacement, Highway MPG, and Vehicle Class")
```

4. Faceting

Faceting is a technique that allows you to create multiple panels based on the levels of a categorical variable. This is useful for comparing distributions across groups.

```R
```

```
ggplot(mpg, aes(x = displ, y = hwy)) + geom_point() +
facet_wrap(~ class)
```
```

This command will create a separate scatterplot for each vehicle class.

We have explored the fundamental features of ggplot2 in R programming, covering how to create basic visualizations, customize them, and use faceting for better insights. The capabilities of ggplot2 extend far beyond what we have covered here, allowing for the creation of complex and informative visualizations.

To truly master ggplot2, practice is key. Experiment with different datasets and visualizations, and refer to the extensive documentation available online. The ability to turn raw data into compelling visual stories will greatly enhance your data analysis skills and communicate your findings with clarity and impact.

# Visual Techniques to Understand Feature Relationships

This chapter will explore several visual techniques, including scatter plots, heatmaps, pair plots, and more, using the R programming language. With real-world examples and sample code, we aim to empower you with the skills to effectively visualize and understand feature relationships.

## Why Visualize Feature Relationships?

Feature relationships provide insights into how different
```

variables interact with each other. Understanding these interactions is crucial for several reasons:

Pattern Detection: Visualizations can reveal underlying patterns, trends, and anomalies that might not be obvious in raw data.

Outliers Identification: Certain features might demonstrate outlier behavior when visualized, helping with data cleaning and preprocessing.

Hypothesis Generation: Visuals can help generate hypotheses regarding relationships between features that can be further tested using statistical methods.

Modeling Assistance: When building predictive models, understanding feature interactions aids in selecting the right features and understanding their collective influence.

1. Scatter Plots ### Overview

Scatter plots are one of the simplest and most effective ways to visualize the relationship between two quantitative variables. Each point represents an observation, with the X and Y axes corresponding to two different features.

Implementation

```R
# Load necessary libraries library(ggplot2)

# Sample dataset data(mtcars)

# Creating a scatter plot ggplot(mtcars, aes(x = wt, y = mpg)) + geom_point(color = "blue") +

labs(title = "Scatter Plot of Weight vs MPG", x = "Weight
```

(1000 lbs)",

y = "Miles per Gallon (MPG)") + theme_minimal()
```

### Interpretation

In this example, the relationship between `weight` (wt) and `miles per gallon` (mpg) is visually represented. A negative trend is often observed, indicating that heavier cars tend to have lower fuel efficiency.

## 2. Correlation Matrices with Heatmaps ### Overview

A correlation matrix displays the pair-wise correlation coefficients between features in a dataset. Visualizing it using a heatmap can provide an immediate sense of the relationships between multiple variables.

### Implementation

```R
# Load necessary libraries library(reshape2)

# Compute correlation matrix cor_matrix <- cor(mtcars)

# Create heatmap heatmap(cor_matrix,

main = "Correlation Heatmap of mtcars",

col = colorRampPalette(c("blue", "white", "red"))(20), margin = c(10, 10))
```

Interpretation

In the heatmap, darker shades indicate stronger correlations. For instance, you might observe that `hp`
```

(horsepower) and `mpg` are negatively correlated, suggesting that increased horsepower is associated with lower miles per gallon.

3. Pair Plots ### Overview

Pair plots provide a grid of scatterplots for each pair of features in a dataset. This technique offers a comprehensive view of relationships among all features and is particularly valuable when working with multidimensional data.

Implementation

```R
# Load necessary libraries library(GGally)
# Create pair plot ggpairs(mtcars,
aes(color = factor(cyl)),
title = "Pair Plot of mtcars Dataset")
```

Interpretation

The pair plot illustrates relationships for all pairs of features, while groups are differentiated by cylinder count (`cyl`). This can highlight how different groups behave distinctly across multiple dimensions.

4. Box Plots for Categorical Relationships ### Overview

Box plots are effective for understanding the relationship between a categorical feature and a continuous feature. They provide a visual summary of the distribution, highlighting medians and quartiles.

Implementation

```R
# Creating a box plot

ggplot(mtcars, aes(x = factor(cyl), y = mpg)) +
geom_boxplot(fill = "lightblue") +

labs(title = "Box Plot of MPG by Cylinder Count", x = "Number of Cylinders",

y = "Miles per Gallon (MPG)") + theme_minimal()
```

The box plot shows the distribution of `miles per gallon` across different cylinder counts. It allows for easy comparison of medians and variability among groups.

Visual techniques are indispensable tools for understanding feature relationships in R programming. From scatter plots to heatmaps and pair plots, each method offers unique insights into how features interact. By harnessing the power of visualization, analysts can make more informed decisions, detect patterns, and generate hypotheses from complex datasets.

Chapter 5: Introduction to Machine Learning Concepts

In this chapter, we will explore the foundational concepts of machine learning, demystify its terminology, and understand how it fits into the broader field of artificial intelligence.

5.1 What is Machine Learning?

At its core, machine learning is a subset of artificial intelligence (AI) that focuses on the development of algorithms that allow computers to learn from and make predictions or decisions based on data. Unlike traditional programming, where explicit rules dictate how a task is accomplished, machine learning enables systems to improve their performance as they encounter more data.

Machine learning can be broadly categorized into three types:

Supervised Learning: In supervised learning, models are trained on labeled datasets, which means that the input data is paired with the correct output. The model learns to map inputs to outputs and can later make predictions on new, unseen data. Common applications include classification tasks (e.g., email spam detection) and regression tasks (e.g., predicting housing prices).

Unsupervised Learning: Unsupervised learning involves training a model on data without labeled responses. The goal here is to discover patterns or groupings within the data. This type of learning is often used in clustering, anomaly detection, and dimensionality reduction. A classic example is customer segmentation, where businesses group customers based on purchasing behavior.

Reinforcement Learning: Reinforcement learning differs from the previous two methods as it focuses on training agents to make a series of decisions. An agent interacts with an environment, receives feedback in the form of rewards or penalties, and learns to optimize its actions over time. This approach is common in robotics, gaming, and adaptive control systems.

5.2 Key Components of Machine Learning

To effectively understand machine learning, it's essential to discuss the key components that contribute to the success of ML models:

Data: Data is the lifeblood of machine learning. The quality, quantity, and representativeness of the dataset greatly influence the model's performance. Data must be pre-processed and cleaned to ensure that it is usable for training. This includes handling missing values, normalizing data, and encoding categorical variables.

Algorithms: Algorithms are the mathematical models that underlie machine learning. There are various algorithms tailored for different types of problems, including decision trees, neural networks, support vector machines, and k-means clustering. Choosing the right algorithm depends on the specific task and the nature of the data.

Features: Features refer to the individual measurable properties or characteristics used by the model to learn from the data. Feature selection and extraction are crucial steps in the machine learning pipeline, as the right features can significantly improve model accuracy while

71

irrelevant or redundant features can detract from performance.

Model Training and Evaluation: After selecting the appropriate algorithm and features, the next step is to train the model using the training dataset. This involves adjusting model parameters to minimize error and improve predictions. Once the model is trained, it is evaluated using validation and test datasets to assess its generalization performance.

5.3 The Machine Learning Workflow

Machine learning is not a straightforward process; it involves a structured workflow. Here's an overview of the typical steps in a machine learning project:

Problem Definition: Clearly define the problem you aim to solve and the objectives of the project.

Data Collection: Gather relevant data from various sources, including databases, APIs, or web scraping.

Data Preparation: Pre-process the data by cleaning, transforming, and organizing it for analysis.

Feature Engineering: Select, create, and transform features that will be used for training the model.

Model Selection: Choose the appropriate machine learning algorithm based on the problem type and data characteristics.

Training: Train the model on the prepared dataset, adjusting parameters to find the best fit.

Evaluation: Evaluate the model's performance using

appropriate metrics (like accuracy, precision, recall, or F1 score) and ensure it generalizes well to unseen data.

Deployment: Deploy the model into a production environment where it can make predictions on new data.

Monitoring and Maintenance: Continuously monitor the model's performance and update it as necessary based on new data or changing conditions.

5.4 Real-World Applications of Machine Learning

Machine learning has diverse applications across industries, demonstrating its potential to solve complex problems. Here are a few notable examples:

Healthcare: ML algorithms are used in predictive analytics to identify disease outbreaks, assist in medical imaging, and personalize treatment plans for patients.

Finance: In the banking sector, machine learning powers fraud detection systems, risk assessment models, and algorithmic trading strategies.

Retail: E-commerce platforms utilize recommendation engines powered by ML to tailor product suggestions to individual customers, enhancing user experience and increasing sales.

Manufacturing: Predictive maintenance powered by ML can forecast when equipment will fail, allowing for timely interventions that reduce downtime and costs.

As we conclude this introduction to machine learning concepts, it is evident that machine learning has revolutionized how we approach problems and make data-driven decisions across various domains. With a solid understanding of its fundamental principles, you are better equipped to delve deeper into this fascinating field.

Supervised vs Unsupervised Learning

While both methods play crucial roles in data analysis, they serve different purposes and operate on different principles. In this chapter, we will delve into the distinctions between supervised and unsupervised learning, explore how they can be implemented in R programming, and illustrate their applications with practical examples.

1. Understanding Supervised Learning

Supervised learning involves using a labeled dataset to train a model, where the algorithm learns to predict an outcome based on input features. In fully labeled datasets, each training example is paired with an output label. The model learns from this data and is then able to make predictions on unseen data.

1.1 Key Features of Supervised Learning

Labeled Data: Requires a dataset where the input features and corresponding output labels are known.

Prediction: The primary goal is to predict the output for new, unseen data.

Common Algorithms: Include linear regression, logistic regression, decision trees, support vector machines, and neural networks.

1.2 Applications of Supervised Learning

Supervised learning is widely used in applications such as:

Spam Detection: Classifying emails as spam or not

spam based on historical data.

Credit Scoring: Predicting whether a loan will default based on past records.

House Price Prediction: Estimating property values based on features like location, size, and amenities.

1.3 Implementing Supervised Learning in R

R provides robust packages for implementing supervised learning. Below is an example using the `caret` package for a classification task.

```R
# Load necessary libraries library(caret) library(ggplot2)

# Load the iris dataset data(iris)

# Split the dataset into training and testing sets set.seed(123)

trainIndex <- createDataPartition(iris$Species, p = .7, list = FALSE,

times = 1) irisTrain <- iris[trainIndex, ] irisTest <- iris[-trainIndex, ]


# Train a decision tree model

model <- train(Species ~ ., data = irisTrain, method = "rpart")

# Make predictions

predictions <- predict(model, irisTest)

# Confusion matrix confusionMatrix(predictions, irisTest$Species)
```

```
```

2. Understanding Unsupervised Learning

Unsupervised learning, in contrast, does not use labeled data. Instead, it explores the inherent structure of the data by identifying patterns and groupings based on the features alone. The primary objective is to discover hidden structures without prior knowledge of the outputs.

2.1 Key Features of Unsupervised Learning

Unlabeled Data: Operates on datasets where no labels are provided.

Pattern Discovery: Aims to find hidden patterns, clusters, or associations in the data.

Common Algorithms: Include k-means clustering, hierarchical clustering, and principal component analysis (PCA).

2.2 Applications of Unsupervised Learning

Unsupervised learning is utilized in various scenarios, such as:

Customer Segmentation: Grouping customers based on purchasing behavior without predefined categories.

Anomaly Detection: Identifying fraudulent transactions by detecting outliers in transaction data.

Market Basket Analysis: Discovering purchase patterns based on the items added to shopping carts. ### 2.3 Implementing Unsupervised Learning in R

Similarly, R is equipped for unsupervised learning tasks. Below is an example using k-means clustering to partition the iris dataset.

```R
# Load necessary libraries library(ggplot2)

# Use only numerical features for clustering iris_numeric
<- iris[, -5]

# Perform k-means clustering set.seed(123)

kmeans_result <- kmeans(iris_numeric, centers = 3,
nstart = 20)

# Add cluster results to the original dataset iris$Cluster <-
as.factor(kmeans_result$cluster)

# Visualize the clusters

ggplot(iris, aes(x = Sepal.Length, y = Sepal.Width, color =
Cluster)) + geom_point(size = 3) +

labs(title = "K-Means Clustering of Iris Data") +


theme_minimal()
```

3. Key Differences Between Supervised and Unsupervised Learning

Understanding the differences between these two approaches is crucial for selecting the appropriate technique for a given problem.

Feature	Supervised Learning	Unsupervised Learning

| Data Type | Requires labeled data | Uses unlabeled data |

| Goal | Predict an outcome based on input features | Discover patterns and structures in the data |

| Algorithms | Regression, Classification| Clustering, Association, Dimensionality Reduction |

| Output | Output variable(s) predicted | Groupings or representations |

| Learning Method | Guided learning (with guidance from labels) | Discovery-oriented (no labels)

|

In summary, supervised and unsupervised learning are two fundamental paradigms in machine learning, each with its own methodologies, applications, and use cases. R programming provides a comprehensive toolkit to implement both approaches, empowering data scientists and analysts to glean valuable insights from their datasets. By mastering these techniques, practitioners can tackle a variety of real-world problems, ranging from predicting outcomes to uncovering hidden relationships within the data.

Key ML Terms: Features, Labels, Overfitting, Underfitting

This chapter delves into key terms such as features, labels, overfitting, and underfitting, explaining their significance in the context of machine learning using R programming.

Features and Labels ### Features

In machine learning, **features** are the individual measurable properties or characteristics of the data used to make predictions. During data collection, various attributes are made available for analysis, which are summarized in a dataset. In R, features can be represented in various forms, including numerical values, categorical data, or text.

For example, consider a dataset for predicting house prices. The features might include:

Square footage

Number of bedrooms

Location (categorical variable)

Age of the house

In R, a feature matrix can be created using data frames, where each row corresponds to an observation, and each column corresponds to a feature. Here's how you might create a basic data frame:

```R
# Creating a data frame for house prices houses <- data.frame(
square_footage = c(1500, 2000, 2500, 1800),
bedrooms = c(3, 4, 4, 3),
location = c('Suburb', 'Urban', 'Urban', 'Suburb'), age = c(5, 10, 15, 7)
)
```

Labels

Labels are the outputs or the target values we aim to predict using machine learning models. In the house price example, the label would be the actual price of the houses. Labels correspond to the dependent variable in a supervised learning task, where the model learns the relationship between the features and the labels.

To add labels to the previous example, you can augment the data frame as follows:

```R
# Adding labels to the house prices

houses$price <- c(300000, 450000, 600000, 350000)
```

The dataset now contains both features and labels, allowing you to begin training a model.

Overfitting

Overfitting occurs when a machine learning model learns not only the underlying pattern in the training dataset but also the noise, resulting in a model that performs exceptionally well on training data but poorly on unseen data. This happens when the model is too complex, containing too many parameters relative to the number of observations.

How to Detect Overfitting

One common method to detect overfitting is by splitting your data into training and testing sets. You train your model on the training set and evaluate its performance on the testing set. Discrepancies between high training accuracy and low testing accuracy indicate potential overfitting.

Example in R

Here's how to visualize overfitting using a simple linear regression model with polynomial terms.

```R
# Load necessary library library(ggplot2)

# Generate synthetic data set.seed(42)

x <- seq(-3, 3, length.out = 100)

y <- 2 * x^2 + rnorm(100)  # Quadratic relationship with noise

# Create a training and testing set train_indices <- sample(1:100, size = 70)

train_data <- data.frame(x = x[train_indices], y = y[train_indices])  test_data <- data.frame(x = x[-train_indices], y = y[-train_indices])

# Fit a polynomial regression model

model <- lm(y ~ poly(x, 10), data = train_data)  # Overly complex model

# Predictions

train_preds <- predict(model, newdata = train_data)  test_preds <- predict(model, newdata = test_data)

# Compare training and testing performances

train_rmse <- sqrt(mean((train_data$y - train_preds)^2))  test_rmse <- sqrt(mean((test_data$y - test_preds)^2))
```

```
print(paste("Training          RMSE:",          train_rmse))
print(paste("Testing RMSE:", test_rmse))
```

In the above example, you will likely find a low training RMSE but a much higher testing RMSE, indicating overfitting.

Underfitting

Underfitting refers to a scenario where a model is too simplistic to capture the underlying trend in the data adequately. Such models often yield low performance on both the training and testing datasets, suggesting that they are not capturing the necessary complexity of the data.

Example in R

To illustrate underfitting, consider fitting a linear regression model to inherently nonlinear data:

```R
# Fit a linear model (underfitting) linear_model <- lm(y ~ x, data = train_data)
```

Predictions

```
linear_preds <- predict(linear_model, newdata = test_data)
```

Compare the RMSEs

```
linear_test_rmse <- sqrt(mean((test_data$y - linear_preds)^2)) print(paste("Testing RMSE for underfitting model:", linear_test_rmse))
```

```
```

In this case, the RMSE for the linear model will be high because the model fails to capture the quadratic nature of the data.

Understanding the concepts of features, labels, overfitting, and underfitting is vital for anyone entering the field of machine learning. In R programming, these concepts can be effectively manipulated and analyzed to build models that generalize well to new data while maintaining a balance between complexity and simplicity.

Chapter 6: Preparing Data for Machine Learning

In this chapter, we will explore various techniques for preparing data in R programming for machine learning applications. We will cover the following topics:

Understanding Your Data

Data Cleaning

Data Transformation

Feature Engineering

Data Splitting

Standardization and Normalization

Dealing with Categorical Variables

---

1. Understanding Your Data

Before diving into the process of preparing your data, you must first understand what you are working with. This typically involves:

Exploratory Data Analysis (EDA): Use R functions such as `summary()`, `str()`, and visualizations with packages like `ggplot2` to understand the distribution and relationships in your data.

Assessing Data Quality: Look for missing values, duplicates, and outliers. The `dplyr` package can help you manipulate and summarize your data effectively.

Example:

```R
library(dplyr)
```

```
data <- read.csv("your_dataset.csv") summary(data)
str(data)
```

2. Data Cleaning

Data cleaning is essential to enhance the quality of the dataset. Here are common tasks involved in this phase:

Handling Missing Values: You can remove rows with missing values or fill in gaps using techniques like mean imputation or k-nearest neighbors (KNN) imputation using R packages like `missForest`.

```R
library(missForest)
data_clean <- na.roughfix(data)
```

Removing Duplicates: Use `distinct()` from `dplyr` to filter out repeated entries.

```R
data_clean <- distinct(data)
```

Identifying Outliers: Use visualizations such as box plots to detect and address outliers.

```R
boxplot(data$variable)
```

3. Data Transformation

Once the data is clean, you may need to transform it to

better suit your analytical needs. Key aspects include:

Scaling and Normalization: Especially for algorithms sensitive to scale (e.g., K-Means or SVM), the data should be scaled to ensure fair treatment of all features.

```R
data_scaled <- scale(data[, -1])  # Assuming first column is a label
```

Log Transformation: This can be useful for data that spans several orders of magnitude.

```R
data$log_variable <- log(data$variable + 1)
```

4. Feature Engineering

Feature engineering involves creating new features or modifying existing ones to improve model performance. Common techniques include:

Creating Interaction Terms: Combine two or more features to capture relationships.

```R
data$interaction <- data$feature1 * data$feature2
```

Binning Continuous Variables: Convert numerical variables into categorical ones to capture non-linear relationships.

```R
```

```R
data$bins <- cut(data$numerical_variable, breaks=4)
```

Using Domain Knowledge: Incorporate any specific knowledge you might have about the data to create meaningful features.

5. Data Splitting

Before training your machine learning model, you must split your data into training and test sets. This helps in evaluating the model's performance on unseen data:

```R
set.seed(123) # For reproducibility

index <- sample(1:nrow(data_clean), 0.7 * nrow(data_clean)) train_data <- data_clean[index, ]

test_data <- data_clean[-index, ]
```

6. Standardization and Normalization

Two common methods for ensuring feature scaling are standardization (Z-score normalization) and min-max normalization.

Standardization:

```R
data_standardized <- scale(data)
```

Min-Max Normalization:

```R
```

```
data_normalized <- (data - min(data)) / (max(data) -
min(data))
```
```

Standardization is useful when your data is normally
distributed, while Min-Max normalization is effective
when you need features in a specific range (e.g., 0 to 1).

## 7. Dealing with Categorical Variables

Categorical data must be encoded into a numerical format
to be used in machine learning algorithms. Common
methods in R include:

**One-Hot Encoding:** This creates binary columns for
each category within a variable.

```R library(caret)
```

```
data_dummy <- dummyVars(" ~ .", data = data_clean)
data_encoded <- predict(data_dummy, newdata =
data_clean)
```
```

Label Encoding: Assign a unique integer value to each
category.

```R
```
```
data$category <- as.numeric(factor(data$category))
```
```

Data preparation is a vital step in the machine learning
process that is often overlooked. Investing time in
understanding, cleaning, transforming, and engineering
your dataset will yield dividends in terms of model
accuracy and robustness.
```

Feature Engineering and Selection

The quality and relevance of features can significantly influence the performance of a model. This chapter delves into the various techniques and methodologies for feature engineering and selection using R programming, a powerful and open-source language widely used in statistical computing and data analysis.

1. Understanding Feature Engineering

Feature engineering refers to the process of transforming raw data into meaningful inputs that enhance the predictive power of a model. This involves creating new features, transforming existing ones, or selecting a subset of features that contribute most significantly to the outcome variable. In R, various packages and functions facilitate these processes efficiently.

1.1 Importance of Feature Engineering

Model Performance: Well-engineered features can lead to better model performance and accuracy.

Interpretability: Good feature selection enhances model interpretability, making it easier for practitioners to derive business insights.

Dimensionality Reduction: Reducing the number of features helps mitigate overfitting and improves computational efficiency.

2. Techniques for Feature Engineering

Feature engineering techniques can be broadly classified into several categories: #### 2.1 Creating New Features

Creating new features is an essential part of feature engineering. This can be done through:

Arithmetic Operations: Combining existing features using addition, subtraction, multiplication, or division.

Date and Time Features: Extracting year, month, day, hour, etc., from date-time variables.

Binning and Discretization: Converting continuous variables into categorical ones through binning.

Example in R:

```R
library(dplyr) data <- data %>%
mutate(year = as.numeric(format(date_column, "%Y")),
month = as.numeric(format(date_column, "%m")), day =
as.numeric(format(date_column, "%d")), total_sales =
price * quantity)
```

2.2 Transforming Features

Transformations can help normalize data and improve relations between variables:

Logarithmic Transformation: Useful for skewed data.

Scaling: Standardization and normalization techniques.

Example in R:

```R
data$log_sales <- log(data$total_sales + 1) data <-
scale(data[, c("feature1", "feature2")])
```

```
```

2.3 Encoding Categorical Variables

Machine learning algorithms typically require numerical input. Thus, categorical variables must be encoded:

One-Hot Encoding: Creating binary columns for each category.

Label Encoding: Converting categorical labels to numeric.

Example in R:

```R
library(caret)

data <- dummyVars("~.", data = data) data_transformed <- predict(data, newdata = data)
```

3. Feature Selection Strategies

Once features are engineered, the next step is to select the most relevant features. Feature selection can enhance model performance by preventing overfitting and reducing computation time.

3.1 Filter Methods

Filter methods evaluate the relevance of features based on statistical measures.

Correlation Coefficient: Selecting features based on their correlation with the target variable.

Example in R:

```R
```

```R
correlation_matrix <- cor(data)

high_correlation <- findCorrelation(correlation_matrix,
cutoff = 0.75)
```

3.2 Wrapper Methods

Wrapper methods assess the performance of a model based on subsets of features.

Recursive Feature Elimination (RFE): Using cross-validation to identify the best set of features.

Example in R:

```R
library(caret)

control <- rfeControl(method="cv", number=10)

results <- rfe(data[, -target_column], data[, target_column], sizes=c(1:5), rfeControl=control)
```

3.3 Embedded Methods

Embedded methods perform feature selection as part of the model training process.

Lasso Regression: Adds a penalty for having many nonzero coefficients.

Example in R:

```R
library(glmnet)

x <- model.matrix(target ~ ., data = data)[, -1] y <- data$target
```

```
lasso_model <- glmnet(x, y, alpha = 1)
```
```

### 4. Evaluating Feature Importance

Evaluating feature importance can inform decisions about which features to keep:

**Tree-Based Methods**: Feature importance can be extracted from tree-based methods like random forests or gradient boosting.

**Example in R**:
```R
library(randomForest)

rf_model <- randomForest(target ~ ., data = data)
importance(rf_model)
```

Feature engineering and selection are foundational components of building effective machine learning models in R programming. By creatively transforming and selecting features, data scientists can significantly enhance model accuracy, interpretability, and overall performance.

Data Normalization and Handling Missing Values

Two fundamental aspects of data preprocessing are data normalization and handling missing values. This chapter will guide you through the concepts, techniques, and practical implementations of these processes in R programming.

Section 1: Understanding Data Normalization

93
```

Data normalization refers to the process of transforming data into a format that is consistent and standardized. This helps in improving the performance and accuracy of machine learning algorithms by ensuring that features contribute equally to the distance calculations, particularly in distance-based algorithms such as K-Nearest Neighbors (KNN) and clustering methods.

1.1 Why Normalize Data?

Data normalization is crucial for several reasons:

Feature Scale: Features measured on different scales can adversely affect the model's performance.

Distance Measurement: Algorithms that rely on distance calculations require normalized data to ensure fair comparisons.

Gradient Descent: Normalized data can help in faster convergence during the optimization process.

1.2 Common Normalization Techniques

There are several techniques for normalizing data, including:

1.2.1 Min-Max Normalization

This technique rescales the feature to a fixed range, typically [0, 1].

\[
X_{norm} = \frac{X - X_{min}}{X_{max} - X_{min}}
\]

Implementation in R:

```R
```

```R
normalize_min_max <- function(x) { return((x - min(x)) /
(max(x) - min(x)))
}

data_normalized       <-       as.data.frame(lapply(data,
normalize_min_max))
```

1.2.2 Z-Score Standardization

Z-score normalization scales the features based on the
mean and standard deviation.

$$
Z = \frac{X - \mu}{\sigma}
$$

Implementation in R:

```R
normalize_z_score <- function(x) { return((x - mean(x)) /
sd(x))
}

data_standardized       <-       as.data.frame(lapply(data,
normalize_z_score))
```

1.3 Considerations for Normalization

Outliers: Outliers can skew the results of
normalization, particularly with Min-Max normalization.
Consider removing or capping outliers before
normalization.

Feature Distribution: Examine the distribution of
95

your data. For skewed distributions, consider log or power transformations before normalization.

Section 2: Handling Missing Values

Missing values are a common occurrence in real-world datasets, and how you deal with them can significantly influence the outcomes of your analysis.

2.1 Types of Missing Data

MCAR (Missing Completely at Random): The likelihood of a data point being missing is independent of any observed or unobserved data.

MAR (Missing at Random): The missingness is related to observed data but not to the values of the missing data.

MNAR (Missing Not at Random): The missingness is related to the missing value itself.

2.2 Approaches to Handle Missing Values

There are several strategies to handle missing data, each with its implications.

2.2.1 Deletion Methods

Listwise Deletion: Remove any row with missing values.

Implementation in R:
```R
data_complete <- na.omit(data)
```

Pairwise Deletion: Use available data without eliminating entire cases. #### 2.2.2 Imputation Methods

Mean/Median Imputation: Replacing missing values with the mean or median of the feature.

Implementation in R:

```R
data[is.na(data$feature)] <- mean(data$feature, na.rm = TRUE)
```

K-Nearest Neighbors Imputation: Using the KNN algorithm to estimate missing values based on similarities with other data points.

Multiple Imputation: Generating multiple imputed datasets, analyzing each, and pooling the results. #### 2.2.3 Advanced Methods

Predictive Models: Using regression models to predict missing values based on other available

predictors.

Deep Learning Approaches: Techniques like autoencoders can also be explored for complex datasets. ### 2.3 Assessing Imputation Methods

It's essential to evaluate the effectiveness of imputation methods. You can use measures like Mean Absolute Error (MAE) or Root Mean Square Error (RMSE) to assess how well your imputed values perform relative to actual values.

Data normalization and handling missing values are foundational preprocessing steps in R programming that enhance the quality of datasets and the robustness of models. By applying techniques such as Min-Max normalization, Z-Score standardization, and thoughtful imputation methods, you can ensure that your analyses yield reliable and actionable insights. Investing time in these practices will pay dividends in the accuracy and interpretability of your results.

Chapter 7: Supervised Learning - Regression Techniques

In this chapter, we will explore regression techniques using the R programming language, focusing on linear regression, polynomial regression, and regularized regression methods.

Understanding Regression

Regression analysis aims to establish the relationship between a dependent variable (target) and one or more independent variables (predictors). The simplest form is linear regression, where the relationship is represented by a straight line.

The general formula for a linear regression model is:

$$
y = \beta_0 + \beta_1 x_1 + \beta_2 x_2 + \ldots + \beta_n x_n + \epsilon
$$

Where:

y is the dependent variable.

$x_1, x_2, \ldots, x_n$ are the independent variables.

β_0 is the intercept of the line.

$\beta_1, \beta_2, \ldots, \beta_n$ are the coefficients for each independent variable.

ϵ is the error term.

Setting up R for Regression Analysis

Before we start, ensure you have R and RStudio installed

on your system. If not, download and install them from the [R Project](https://www.r-project.org/) and [RStudio](https://rstudio.com/) websites, respectively.

In this chapter, we will use built-in datasets and libraries like `tidyverse` for data manipulation and visualization, and `ggplot2` for plotting our results.

```r
# Install required packages install.packages("tidyverse")
install.packages("ggplot2")

# Load libraries library(tidyverse) library(ggplot2)
```

Linear Regression in R ### Dataset Preparation

We will use the built-in `mtcars` dataset for our regression examples. This dataset contains information about various car models, including miles per gallon (mpg), number of cylinders, horsepower, and more.

```r
# Inspect the mtcars dataset head(mtcars)
```

Building a Linear Regression Model

To predict miles per gallon (mpg) based on horsepower (hp), we can build a linear regression model using the `lm()` function:

```r
# Linear regression model
```

```
linear_model <- lm(mpg ~ hp, data = mtcars)
```
Summary of the model summary(linear_model)
```
```

The summary output provides essential statistics, including the coefficients, R-squared value, and p-values. R-squared indicates the proportion of variance in the dependent variable that can be explained by the independent variables.

Visualizing the Results

To visualize our regression line, we can use `ggplot2` to plot the original data along with the predicted values:

```r
# Visualization
ggplot(mtcars, aes(x = hp, y = mpg)) + geom_point() +
geom_smooth(method = "lm", col = "blue") + labs(title =
"Linear Regression: MPG vs. Horsepower",
x = "Horsepower",
y = "Miles Per Gallon (MPG)")
```

Polynomial Regression

In some cases, the relationship between the independent and dependent variables is non-linear. Polynomial regression allows us to fit a polynomial equation to the data.

Fitting a Polynomial Model

We can fit a polynomial regression model by including

101

higher powers of the predictor variable. Let's fit a second-degree polynomial to the mpg data:

```r
# Polynomial regression model
poly_model <- lm(mpg ~ poly(hp, 2), data = mtcars)
# Summary of the polynomial model
summary(poly_model)
```

Visualizing Polynomial Regression

As before, we can visualize this polynomial regression:

```r
# Visualization of polynomial regression ggplot(mtcars,
aes(x = hp, y = mpg)) + geom_point() +
geom_smooth(method = "lm", formula = y ~ poly(x, 2),
col = "red") + labs(title = "Polynomial Regression: MPG
vs. Horsepower",
x = "Horsepower",
y = "Miles Per Gallon (MPG)")
```

Regularized Regression Techniques

When dealing with high-dimensional datasets, regularization techniques like Ridge and Lasso regression can prevent overfitting by adding a penalty term to the loss function.

Ridge Regression

Ridge regression applies L2 regularization, which adds the squared magnitude of coefficients as a penalty term.

```r
# Load necessary library install.packages("glmnet")
library(glmnet)

# Prepare the data

x <- as.matrix(mtcars[, -1]) # All the predictor variables y <- mtcars[, 1] # Dependent variable (mpg)

# Fit a ridge regression model ridge_model <- glmnet(x, y, alpha = 0)

# To visualize coefficients plot(ridge_model, xvar = "lambda")
```

Lasso Regression

Lasso regression, on the other hand, uses L1 regularization, which can shrink some coefficients to zero, effectively selecting a simpler model.

```r
# Fit a lasso regression model lasso_model <- glmnet(x, y, alpha = 1)

# To visualize coefficients plot(lasso_model, xvar = "lambda")
```

Cross-Validation for Regularization

To choose the best regularization parameter (λ), we can use cross-validation.

```r
r set.seed(123)
cv_model <- cv.glmnet(x, y)
# Best lambda value
best_lambda <- cv_model$lambda.min best_lambda
```

We explored the fundamental concepts of regression techniques in R programming within the context of supervised learning. We examined linear regression for straightforward relationships, polynomial regression for complex non-linear patterns, and regularized regression methods like Ridge and Lasso for high- dimensional data.

Linear and Multiple Linear Regression in R

Linear regression aims to model the relationship between one dependent variable and one or more independent variables by fitting a linear equation to the observed data. In this chapter, we will explore both simple linear regression and multiple linear regression using R, a popular programming language and software suite for statistical computing and data analysis.

1. Simple Linear Regression ### 1.1 Concept

Simple linear regression is used when we want to predict the value of a dependent variable, Y, based on the value of one independent variable, X. The relationship is expressed in the form:

\[

$Y = \beta_0 + \beta_1 X + \epsilon$

\]

Where:

\(Y\) is the dependent variable.

\(X\) is the independent variable.

\(\beta_0\) is the y-intercept.

\(\beta_1\) is the slope of the line, indicating how much \(Y\) changes for a one-unit change in \(X\).

\(\epsilon\) is the error term that accounts for the variability in \(Y\) not explained by \(X\). ### 1.2 Fitting a Simple Linear Regression Model in R

To illustrate simple linear regression in R, let's consider a dataset of cars where we want to analyze the relationship between the horsepower of the car (independent variable) and its price (dependent variable).

Step 1: Load necessary libraries and dataset

```R
# Load necessary libraries library(ggplot2)
# Sample dataset cars <- data.frame(
horsepower = c(100, 150, 200, 250, 300, 350),
price = c(20000, 25000, 30000, 35000, 40000, 45000)
)
```

Step 2: Fit the model

```R
# Fit the simple linear regression model model_simple <-
```

```
lm(price ~ horsepower, data = cars)
summary(model_simple)
```

Step 3: Visualize the results

```R
# Plot the data points and the regression line ggplot(cars,
aes(x = horsepower, y = price)) +

geom_point() +

geom_smooth(method = "lm", col = "blue") +

labs(title = "Simple Linear Regression: Price vs.
Horsepower", x = "Horsepower",

y = "Price")
```

2. Multiple Linear Regression ### 2.1 Concept

Multiple linear regression is an extension of simple linear regression. It models the relationship between one dependent variable and multiple independent variables. The general form is:

$$
Y = \beta_0 + \beta_1X_1 + \beta_2X_2 + ... + \beta_nX_n + \epsilon
$$

Where:

$(X_1, X_2, ... X_n)$ are the independent variables.

The other symbols retain the same meaning as in simple linear regression. ### 2.2 Fitting a Multiple Linear Regression Model in R

Continuing with our dataset, let's add an additional independent variable, such as the weight of the car, to see how both horsepower and weight influence the price.

Step 1: Expand the dataset

```R
# Expand the dataset
cars$weight <- c(1500, 1600, 1700, 1800, 1900, 2000)
```

Step 2: Fit the multiple linear regression model

```R
# Fit the multiple linear regression model
model_multiple <- lm(price ~ horsepower + weight, data = cars) summary(model_multiple)
```

Step 3: Assessing the model

Using the `summary()` function, we can assess the model fit, looking for:

Coefficients of the model.

R-squared value (indicating how well the independent variables explain the variability in the dependent variable).

p-values for each coefficient (to assess their significance).

3. Diagnostics and Assumptions

Regression analysis comes with certain assumptions that must be validated:

Linearity: The relationship between the dependent and independent variables should be linear.

Independence: Observations should be independent of each other.

Homoscedasticity: The residual errors should have constant variance.

Normality: The residuals should be normally distributed.

We can visually check some of these assumptions using diagnostic plots. ### Step 4: Diagnostic Plots

```R
# Diagnostic plots for the multiple linear regression model
par(mfrow = c(2, 2))

plot(model_multiple)
```

These plots help identify potential problems with our model, such as non-linearity, non-constant variance, or outliers.

We explored simple and multiple linear regression, using R to fit models and visualize results. We learned how to interpret the coefficients and conduct diagnostic checks. Regression analysis serves as a fundamental tool in statistical modeling, offering insights across various fields, from economics to engineering. Practice is key to mastering these techniques, so experiment with different datasets to further your understanding!

Model Evaluation: MSE, RMSE, and Cross-Validation

Different metrics exist to assess how well a model performs, among which Mean Squared Error (MSE) and Root Mean Squared Error (RMSE) are commonly employed in regression analysis. Additionally, methods like Cross-Validation provide a robust framework for evaluating model performance, mitigating overfitting, and ensuring models generalize well to new, unseen data.

In this chapter, we will explore the concepts of MSE, RMSE, and Cross-Validation, emphasizing their significance and implementation in R programming. By the end of this chapter, you will comprehend how to utilize these metrics to evaluate your models effectively.

1. Understanding MSE and RMSE ### 1.1 Mean Squared Error (MSE)

Mean Squared Error (MSE) quantifies the average of the squares of the errors—that is, the average squared difference between the predicted values and the actual values. It is defined mathematically as:

$$
MSE = \frac{1}{n} \sum_{i=1}^{n} (y_i - \hat{y}_i)^2
$$

Where:

n is the number of observations,

109

(y_i) is the actual value,

$(\hat{y}_i)$ is the predicted value.

A smaller MSE value indicates a better fit between predicted and actual values. ### 1.2 Root Mean Squared Error (RMSE)

Root Mean Squared Error (RMSE) is the square root of MSE. It offers the advantage of being in the same units as the response variable, making it easier to interpret. RMSE is defined as follows:

\[

RMSE = \sqrt{MSE} = \sqrt{\frac{1}{n} \sum_{i=1}^{n} (y_i - \hat{y}_i)^2}

\]

RMSE provides not only a sense of the magnitude of the errors but also contains information about their distribution; therefore, it is often preferred for performance evaluation in regression contexts.

2. Implementing MSE and RMSE in R

In R, calculating MSE and RMSE is straightforward. Below is a simple example demonstrating how to use these metrics in R.

```R

# Sample data creation set.seed(42)
```

```r
n <- 100

actual_values <- rnorm(n, mean=50, sd=10)   # Actual values

predicted_values <- actual_values + rnorm(n, mean=0, sd=5) # Predicted values with some noise

# Function to calculate MSE

calculate_mse <- function(actual, predicted) {
mean((actual - predicted)^2)
}

# Function to calculate RMSE

calculate_rmse <- function(actual, predicted) {
sqrt(calculate_mse(actual, predicted))
}

# Calculate MSE and RMSE

mse <- calculate_mse(actual_values, predicted_values)
rmse <- calculate_rmse(actual_values, predicted_values)

cat("Mean Squared Error:", mse, "\n") cat("Root Mean Squared Error:", rmse, "\n")
```
```

## 3. Cross-Validation

Cross-Validation is a powerful statistical method used to estimate the skill of machine learning models. It involves partitioning the data into subsets, training the model on one subset (training set), and testing it on another (validation set). By repeating this process multiple times, Cross-Validation provides a more reliable estimate of model performance.
```

3.1 Types of Cross-Validation

K-Fold Cross-Validation: The dataset is divided into 'K' subsets (folds). The model is trained on \(K-1

\) folds and validated on the remaining fold. This is repeated K times, with each fold being used as the validation set once.

Leave-One-Out Cross-Validation (LOOCV): A special case of K-Fold Cross-Validation where K equals the number of observations. Each iteration uses all but one observation for training.

Stratified Cross-Validation: A variation of K-Fold that preserves the percentage of samples for each class in the dataset, which is especially useful for imbalanced datasets.

3.2 Implementing Cross-Validation in R

The `caret` package in R simplifies the process of performing Cross-Validation. Below is an example of K-Fold Cross-Validation in R:

```R
library(caret)

# Define control method for 10-fold Cross-Validation
control <- trainControl(method = "cv", number = 10)

# Define a simple linear model

model    <-    train(y    =    actual_values,    x    =    data.frame(predicted_values),


method = "lm", trControl = control)

# Print out the results print(model)
```

3.3 Evaluating Model Performance Using Cross-Validation

Using Cross-Validation not only helps in evaluating model performance but also provides insight into how well the model is expected to perform when applied to an independent dataset. The resampling approach reduces the variance associated with a single split of the dataset, ensuring a more reliable estimate.

Understanding and quantifying model evaluation metrics is an essential aspect of building reliable predictive models. Mean Squared Error (MSE) and Root Mean Squared Error (RMSE) provide clear, quantifiable measures of model performance. Furthermore, Cross-Validation offers a robust framework for assessing model generalizability by utilizing multiple segments of the dataset. Implementing these methodologies in R programming provides an efficient and effective way to ensure the quality and reliability of your predictive models.

Chapter 8: Supervised Learning - Classification Techniques

This chapter will delve into supervised learning, specifically focusing on classification techniques implemented in R programming. We'll introduce the concepts of classification, explore various algorithms, and provide practical examples that will help ensure a solid understanding of the topic.

8.1 Overview of Supervised Learning

Supervised learning is a type of machine learning where models are trained on a labeled dataset, meaning that each training instance consists of input features and corresponding output labels. The goal of supervised learning is to learn a mapping from the input data to the output labels so that the model can predict the labels for unseen data.

In the realm of supervised learning, classification is concerned with predicting categorical labels. For instance, given a dataset of email messages, a classification model could be trained to distinguish between spam and non-spam emails.

8.2 Classification Techniques

There are several classification techniques commonly used in R programming, including but not limited to:

Logistic Regression

Decision Trees

Random Forests

Support Vector Machines (SVM)

K-Nearest Neighbors (KNN)

Neural Networks

8.2.1 Logistic Regression

Logistic Regression is a statistical method for predicting binary classes. It models the probability of a default category (label = 1) based on given independent variables.

Implementation in R:

```R
# Load necessary library library(ggplot2)

# Load dataset data(mtcars)

# Logistic regression model to predict the probability of a car being automatic (vs = 1) model <- glm(vs ~ wt + hp, data = mtcars, family = 'binomial')

# Summary of the model summary(model)
```

8.2.2 Decision Trees

A Decision Tree is a flowchart-like structure where each internal node represents a feature (attribute), each branch represents a decision rule, and each leaf node represents an outcome. It is easy to visualize and interpret.

Implementation in R:

```R
library(rpart) library(rpart.plot)

# Fit a decision tree model

tree_model <- rpart(vs ~ wt + hp, data = mtcars)

# Visualization rpart.plot(tree_model)
```

```
```

8.2.3 Random Forests

Random Forest is an ensemble technique that builds multiple decision trees and merges them to achieve better accuracy and control overfitting.

Implementation in R:

```R
library(randomForest)

# Fit a Random Forest model

rf_model <- randomForest(vs ~ wt + hp, data = mtcars, ntree = 100)

# View the importance of variables importance(rf_model)
```

8.2.4 Support Vector Machines (SVM)

Support Vector Machines are a set of supervised learning methods used for classification and regression analysis. They work by finding the hyperplane that best divides a dataset into classes.

Implementation in R:

```R
library(e1071)

# Fit SVM model

svm_model <- svm(vs ~ wt + hp, data = mtcars)

# Plot the SVM model

plot(svm_model, data = mtcars, wt ~ hp, slice = list(hp = 100))
```

8.2.5 K-Nearest Neighbors (KNN)

K-Nearest Neighbors is a non-parametric method that classifies instances based on the majority class among the k-nearest neighbors in the feature space.

Implementation in R:

```R
library(class)
```

Preparing data for KNN set.seed(123)

train_indices <- sample(1:nrow(mtcars), nrow(mtcars) * 0.7) train_data <- mtcars[train_indices,]

test_data <- mtcars[-train_indices,]

Normalizing features for KNN

train_scaled <- scale(train_data[, c("wt", "hp")]) test_scaled <- scale(test_data[, c("wt", "hp")])

KNN model

knn_pred <- knn(train_scaled, test_scaled, train_data$vs, k = 3)

Confusion matrix table(test_data$vs, knn_pred)
```
```

8.2.6 Neural Networks

Neural Networks are advanced computational models inspired by the human brain's structure. They consist of interconnected nodes that process input data and capture complex relationships.

Implementation in R:

```R
library(nnet)
```

Build a neural network model

```
nn_model <- nnet(vs ~ wt + hp, data = mtcars, size = 3,
maxit = 200)
```

Making predictions

```
nn_pred <- predict(nn_model, newdata = test_data, type
= "class")
```
```

## 8.3 Model Evaluation

A critical step in supervised learning is evaluating the
model's performance. Common metrics for classification
include accuracy, precision, recall, F1-score, and ROC-
AUC.

**Confusion Matrix Example in R:**

```R library(caret)
```

Confusion matrix for the logistic regression model

```
predictions <- predict(model, newdata = test_data, type =
"response") confusionMatrix(as.factor(ifelse(predictions >
0.5, 1, 0)), reference = as.factor(test_data$vs))
```


```

We discussed the implementation of several algorithms
such as Logistic Regression, Decision Trees, Random
Forests, SVMs, KNN, and Neural Networks. Furthermore,
we emphasized the importance of model evaluation to
ensure the validity and usefulness of the predictions made
by our models. Mastering these techniques will empower
you to tackle various classification problems and extract
valuable insights from your data.

# Logistic Regression and k-Nearest Neighbors (k-NN)

This chapter aims to provide an in-depth understanding of both techniques, illustrating their implementation in R programming, along with practical examples.

### 1. Logistic Regression #### 1.1 Overview

Logistic regression is a statistical method used for binary classification problems. Unlike linear regression, which predicts continuous outcomes, logistic regression predicts the probability that a given input point belongs to a certain category. The output of a logistic regression model is transformed using the logistic function, which maps any real-valued number into the range of 0 to 1.

#### 1.2 The Logistic Function The logistic function is defined as:

$$
f(z) = \frac{1}{1 + e^{-z}}
$$

where $z$ is the linear combination of the input features. If $p$ is the predicted probability of the positive class, it can be expressed as:

$$
p = f(\beta_0 + \beta_1 x_1 + \beta_2 x_2 + \ldots + \beta_n x_n)
$$

Here, $\beta_0$ is the intercept, and $\beta_1, \beta_2, \ldots, \beta_n$ are the coefficients of the

119

predictor variables $\( x_1, x_2, \ldots, x_n \)$.

#### 1.3 Implementing Logistic Regression in R

To exemplify the implementation of logistic regression in R, we will use the well-known iris dataset. Although this dataset is originally used for multiclass classification, we will simplify it for binary classification by considering only two species of iris flowers.

##### 1.3.1 Data Preparation

```R
# Load necessary libraries library(dplyr) library(ggplot2)

# Load the iris dataset data(iris)


# Create a binary classification based on species
iris_binary <- iris %>% filter(Species != "setosa") %>% mutate(Species = ifelse(Species == "versicolor", 1, 0))

# Display the first few rows head(iris_binary)
```

1.3.2 Fitting the Logistic Regression Model

```R
# Fit the logistic regression model

model <- glm(Species ~ Sepal.Length + Sepal.Width, data = iris_binary, family = binomial)

# Summarize the model summary(model)
```

1.3.3 Model Prediction

```R
# Predict probabilities

predicted_probabilities <- predict(model, type = "response")

# Classify based on a threshold of 0.5

predicted_classes <- ifelse(predicted_probabilities > 0.5, 1, 0)

# Create a confusion matrix

confusion_matrix <- table(Predicted = predicted_classes, Actual = iris_binary$Species) print(confusion_matrix)
```

1.4 Evaluation Metrics

To determine the performance of our logistic regression model, we can calculate various metrics such as accuracy, precision, recall, and F1 score.

```R
# Calculate accuracy

accuracy <- sum(predicted_classes == iris_binary$Species) / nrow(iris_binary) print(paste("Accuracy:", accuracy))
```

2. k-Nearest Neighbors (k-NN) #### 2.1 Overview

k-NN is a non-parametric classification algorithm that classifies instances based on the classes of their nearest neighbors in the feature space. It is simple yet effective, often used when the decision boundary is complex.

121

2.2 How k-NN Works

Select the number of neighbors $\(k \)$.

For each instance to be classified, calculate the distance between the instance and all other instances in the training set.

Sort the distances and select the top $\(k \)$ nearest neighbors.

Assign the most common class among these neighbors to the instance. #### 2.3 Implementing k-NN in R

We will continue with the iris dataset for our k-NN example. ##### 2.3.1 Data Preparation

```R
# Load necessary library library(class)

# Normalize the feature values iris_normalized <- scale(iris_binary[, 1:2])

# Split data into training and testing sets set.seed(123)

train_indices <- sample(1:nrow(iris_normalized), size = 0.8 * nrow(iris_normalized)) train_data <- iris_normalized[train_indices, ]

test_data <- iris_normalized[-train_indices, ] train_labels <- iris_binary$Species[train_indices] test_labels <- iris_binary$Species[-train_indices]
```

2.3.2 Fitting the k-NN Model
```R
# Set value for k k <- 3
```

Predict with k-NN

predictions <- knn(train = train_data, test = test_data, cl = train_labels, k = k)

Create a confusion matrix

knn_confusion_matrix <- table(Predicted = predictions, Actual = test_labels) print(knn_confusion_matrix)
```

#### 2.4 Evaluation Metrics

Similar to logistic regression, we can evaluate the performance of our k-NN model using accuracy and other metrics.

```R

# Calculate accuracy

knn_accuracy <- sum(predictions == test_labels) / length(test_labels)                print(paste("Accuracy:", knn_accuracy))
```

When implemented in R, these techniques provide powerful tools for data scientists to model and predict outcomes based on input features. Logistic regression is suitable for data where the underlying relationship is approximately linear, while k-NN excels with more complex, non-linear relationships.

Decision Trees and Random Forests
```

Decision trees and random forests are two of the most popular algorithms for classification and regression tasks. This chapter will explore the concepts of decision trees and random forests, implementation in R, and practical applications.

1. Decision Trees ### 1.1 Overview

A decision tree is a flowchart-like structure that uses branching methods to illustrate every possible outcome of a decision. Each internal node represents a feature (or attribute), each branch represents a decision rule, and each leaf node represents an outcome (class label).

1.2 Advantages and Disadvantages

Advantages:

Easy to interpret and visualize.

Requires little data preprocessing (no need for normalization or scaling).

Can handle both numerical and categorical data.

Non-parametric, which means no assumptions about the distribution of the data.

Disadvantages:

Prone to overfitting, especially when the tree is deep.

Sensitive to slight variations in data. ### 1.3 Building a Decision Tree in R

To build a decision tree in R, we can use the `rpart` package. Here is a step-by-step guide. #### Step 1: Install and Load Required Packages

```R
                                    install.packages("rpart")
```

```
install.packages("rpart.plot")                    library(rpart)
library(rpart.plot)
```
```

#### Step 2: Prepare the Data

We'll use the built-in `iris` dataset, which contains measurements sepal length, sepal width, petal length, and petal width for three species of flowers.

```R data(iris) head(iris)
```

Step 3: Fit the Decision Tree Model

We will create a decision tree model to classify the species of iris based on the measurements.

```R
# Fitting the decision tree
model <- rpart(Species ~ ., data = iris, method = "class")
# Summary of the model summary(model)
```

Step 4: Visualization

```R
# Plotting the decision tree rpart.plot(model)
```

Step 5: Making Predictions

Now that we have a fitted model, we can make predictions.
```

```R
# Making predictions
predictions <- predict(model, iris, type = "class")
table(predictions, iris$Species)
```

2. Random Forests ### 2.1 Overview

Random forests, an ensemble learning method, combine multiple decision trees to produce a more robust and accurate model. It mitigates the risk of overfitting that is common with individual decision trees.

2.2 Advantages and Disadvantages

Advantages:

Generally more accurate than individual decision trees.

Handles overfitting through averaging.

Provides feature importance scores.

Disadvantages:

Less interpretable than decision trees.

Can be computationally intensive for large datasets. ### 2.3 Building a Random Forest Model in R

To create a random forest model, we can use the `randomForest` package. #### Step 1: Install and Load Required Packages

```R
install.packages("randomForest")
library(randomForest)
```

Step 2: Prepare the Data

We will continue using the `iris` dataset. #### Step 3: Fit the Random Forest Model

```R
# Fitting the random forest model

rf_model <- randomForest(Species ~ ., data = iris, ntree = 100)

# Output the model print(rf_model)
```

Step 4: Making Predictions

We can make predictions using our random forest model.

```R
# Making predictions

rf_predictions        <-        predict(rf_model,        iris)
table(rf_predictions, iris$Species)
```

Step 5: Evaluating Feature Importance

Random forests also allow us to check the importance of features used in the model.

```R
#    Feature    importance    importance(rf_model)
varImpPlot(rf_model)
```

3. Practical Applications ### 3.1 Classification Problems

Both decision trees and random forests are extensively used in classification problems, such as customer segmentation, spam detection, and medical diagnosis.

3.2 Regression Problems

While less common, decision trees and random forests can also handle regression tasks, predicting continuous outcomes based on input variables.

3.3 Feature Selection

Random forests can help in selecting significant features, reducing dimension and improving model performance.

3.4 Handling Imbalanced Datasets

Random forests offer robust solutions for imbalanced datasets, often yielding better results than traditional methods.

Decision trees and random forests are powerful tools in the arsenal of a data scientist. R programming provides suitable libraries for effectively utilizing these models, making them favorable choices for many predictive modeling tasks. As machine learning continues to evolve, mastering these techniques will empower practitioners to solve complex problems in diverse domains.

Chapter 9: Advanced Classification Algorithms

In this chapter, we delve into advanced classification algorithms using R programming, focusing on techniques that can handle complex datasets, incorporate non-linearity, and improve model performance.

9.1 Recap of Basic Classification Algorithms

Before we venture into the advanced territory, let's briefly revisit some of the fundamental classification algorithms covered in previous chapters:

Logistic Regression - A straightforward method for binary classification, offering good interpretability but limited in capturing complex relationships.

K-Nearest Neighbors (KNN) - A non-parametric method that classifies based on proximity to other data points, but can be computationally expensive, especially with large datasets.

Decision Trees - A versatile algorithm that partitions data into subsets based on decision rules, but may suffer from overfitting without careful tuning.

While these foundational algorithms are effective for many applications, they may not suffice in scenarios requiring high accuracy, feature interactions, or when dealing with large volumes of data. Thus, we turn our attention to more sophisticated approaches.

9.2 Support Vector Machines (SVM)

Support Vector Machines are a powerful class of algorithms ideal for binary classification. SVMs work by finding a hyperplane that best separates classes in high-dimensional space. R offers several packages for implementing SVM, notably `e1071` and `kernlab`.

Key Concepts

Kernel Trick: Allows SVM to perform in high-dimensional space without explicitly transforming data. This is particularly useful for non-linear classifications.

Soft Margin: Introduces a penalty for misclassification, allowing SVM to generalize better when dealing with noise.

Implementation Example

```R
# Load necessary library library(e1071)

# Load sample dataset data(iris)

# Split into training and testing sets set.seed(123)

train_indices <- sample(nrow(iris), 0.7 * nrow(iris))
train_data <- iris[train_indices, ]

test_data <- iris[-train_indices, ]

# Train SVM model

svm_model <- svm(Species ~ ., data = train_data, kernel = "radial", cost = 1)

# Make predictions

predictions <- predict(svm_model, test_data)

# Evaluate the model

confusion_matrix <- table(test_data$Species, predictions)
print(confusion_matrix)
```

```
` ` `
```

9.3 Random Forests

Random Forests have gained prominence for their robustness and accuracy. As an ensemble method, they create a multitude of decision trees during training and output the mode of the classes for regression or classification tasks.

Key Advantages

Reducing Overfitting: By averaging multiple trees, random forests can diminish the risk of overfitting, especially in complex datasets.

Feature Importance: Random forests provide estimates of feature importance, which can guide feature selection.

Implementation Example

```R
# Load necessary library library(randomForest)

# Train Random Forest model

rf_model <- randomForest(Species ~ ., data = train_data, ntree = 100)

# Make predictions

rf_predictions <- predict(rf_model, test_data)

# Evaluate the model

rf_confusion_matrix    <-    table(test_data$Species, rf_predictions) print(rf_confusion_matrix)
```

9.4 Gradient Boosting Machines (GBM)

Gradient Boosting Machines have become a go-to method for many data scientists due to their flexibility and power. GBM builds trees sequentially, where each tree helps to correct the errors of the previous ones.

Benefits of GBM

High Predictive Accuracy: Often outperforms other algorithms due to its iterative nature.

Custom Loss Functions: Allows the usage of user-defined loss functions, tailored to specific problems. ### Implementation Example

```R
# Load necessary library library(gbm)


# Train GBM model gbm_model <- gbm(Species ~ .,
data = train_data, distribution = "multinomial", n.trees = 100,
interaction.depth = 3,
n.minobsinnode = 10)
# Make predictions
gbm_predictions <- predict(gbm_model, test_data, n.trees = 100, type = "response") gbm_class <- apply(gbm_predictions, 1, which.max) # Convert probabilities to class labels
# Evaluate the model
gbm_confusion_matrix <- table(test_data$Species,
```

```
levels(iris$Species)[gbm_class])
print(gbm_confusion_matrix)
```
` ` `

9.5 Neural Networks

Neural networks, inspired by the human brain, are incredibly powerful for classification tasks. With libraries like `nnet` and `keras`, R provides accessible paths to create and train neural network models, accommodating complex, non-linear relationships.

Highlights

Multiple Layers: Neural networks can learn hierarchical patterns through multiple layers of nodes.

Regularization Techniques: Techniques like dropout can prevent overfitting, enhancing generalization. ### Implementation Example using the `nnet` package

` ` `R

Load necessary library library(nnet)

Train Neural Network model

```
nn_model <- nnet(Species ~ ., data = train_data, size = 5, maxit = 100)
```

Make predictions

```
nn_predictions <- predict(nn_model, test_data, type = "class")
```

Evaluate the model

```
nn_confusion_matrix <- table(test_data$Species, nn_predictions) print(nn_confusion_matrix)
```

```

## 9.6 Evaluating Model Performance

Once models are trained, evaluating their performance becomes crucial. We utilize metrics such as:

**Accuracy**: Proportion of true results among the total number of cases.

**Precision and Recall**: Particularly useful in imbalanced classes.

**F1 Score**: Represents a balance between precision and recall.

**ROC Curve and AUC**: For visual assessment and comparisons of model performance across multiple thresholds.

We explored advanced classification algorithms, each with its advantages and suitability depending on the problem context. By harnessing the power of Support Vector Machines, Random Forests, Gradient Boosting, and Neural Networks, R programmers can tackle complex classification problems more effectively.

# Support Vector Machines (SVM)

This chapter will introduce the concept of SVMs, discuss their working principles, and demonstrate how to implement SVMs in R programming.

## 1. Introduction to Support Vector Machines

Support Vector Machines are powerful classification
```

algorithms that work by finding the optimal hyperplane which separates data points belonging to different classes. The effectiveness of SVMs stems from their ability to handle both linearly separable and non-linearly separable data through the use of kernel functions.

1.1 Key Concepts

Hyperplane: In an N-dimensional space, a hyperplane is a flat affine subspace of dimension N-1 that separates the data. In a two-dimensional space, this is just a line; in three dimensions, it's a plane.

Support Vectors: These are the data points that lie closest to the hyperplane. They are crucial in determining the position and orientation of the hyperplane. The algorithm maximizes the margin, which is the distance between the hyperplane and the nearest support vectors.

Kernel Trick: The kernel trick allows SVMs to operate in high-dimensional spaces without explicitly transforming the data. By applying a kernel function, SVMs can effectively transform the space and find the optimal hyperplane.

2. Types of SVMs

SVMs can generally be categorized into two types:

Linear SVMs: Used when the data can be separated by a straight line (or hyperplane) without gaps.

Non-linear SVMs: Used when the data classes are not linearly separable. The kernel trick is applied here to map the data into a higher-dimensional space where it becomes linearly separable.

3. Implementing SVMs in R

3.1 Installation of Required Packages

To implement SVMs in R, we typically use the `e1071` package, which provides a straightforward way to build SVM models. If this package isn't already installed, you can do so by running:

```R
install.packages("e1071")
```

3.2 Loading Libraries

Once the package is installed, load it along with any other necessary libraries:

```R
library(e1071)   # For SVM implementation
library(ggplot2) # For visualization
```

3.3 Sample Dataset

For demonstration purposes, we will use the famous iris dataset, which contains three classes of iris plants and four features.

```R
data(iris) # Load iris dataset
head(iris) # Display the first few rows of the dataset
```

3.4 Splitting Data

To evaluate the performance of our SVM model, we need to split the dataset into training and testing sets.

```R
set.seed(123) # For reproducibility

sample_index <- sample(1:nrow(iris), 0.7 * nrow(iris))
train_data <- iris[sample_index, ]

test_data <- iris[-sample_index, ]
```

3.5 Building the SVM Model

Now, we can build our SVM model using the training data. In this example, we will use a linear kernel.

```R
svm_model <- svm(Species ~ ., data = train_data, kernel = "linear") summary(svm_model)
```

3.6 Making Predictions

With our model built, we can now use it to make predictions on the test dataset.

```R
predictions <- predict(svm_model, test_data)
```

3.7 Evaluating the Model

The next step is to evaluate the performance of our model. A common approach is to use a confusion matrix.

```R
confusion_matrix <- table(test_data$Species, predictions)
print(confusion_matrix)
```

The confusion matrix will allow us to visualize the number of correct and incorrect classifications. ### 3.8 Visualization

To gain insights into the decision boundary set by the SVM, we can visualize the results. Although visualizations can be limited in higher dimensions, we can plot two features at a time.

```R
library(ggplot2)
ggplot(data = train_data, aes(x = Sepal.Length, y = Sepal.Width, color = Species)) + geom_point(size = 3) +
stat_contour(data = as.data.frame(predict(svm_model, newdata = expand.grid(Sepal.Length = seq(min(iris$Sepal.Length), max(iris$Sepal.Length), length.out = 100),
Sepal.Width = seq(min(iris$Sepal.Width), max(iris$Sepal.Width),
length.out = 100)))),
aes(z = ..level..), bins = 10) +
theme_minimal() +
ggtitle("SVM Decision Boundary")
```

Support Vector Machines are a robust tool for classification tasks in various domains. With the help of R, implementing SVM models is straightforward and efficient. Understanding SVMs provides a strong foundation for tackling complex data classification problems. As you adapt these techniques to your data, remember to experiment with different kernels (such as polynomial or radial basis function) to improve model performance.

Naive Bayes and Ensemble Methods

This chapter delves into these techniques, exploring their theoretical foundations and practical implementations in R programming. We aim to not only clarify the functioning of Naive Bayes classifiers and ensemble learning but also provide hands-on examples for a better understanding of how they can be effectively used in real-world scenarios.

Section 1: Naive Bayes Classifier ### 1.1 Overview of Naive Bayes

The Naive Bayes classifier is a probabilistic model based on Bayes' theorem, particularly useful for classification tasks. It assumes that the features (or predictors) are conditionally independent given the class label. This simplification, although "naive," often yields remarkably good performance, especially with text classification and spam detection.

1.2 Mathematical Foundation

At its core, Naive Bayes applies Bayes' theorem to calculate the posterior probability of a class given a set of features. Mathematically, it can be expressed as:

\[

$$P(Y|X) = \frac{P(X|Y) \cdot P(Y)}{P(X)}$$

\]

Where:

$P(Y|X)$ is the posterior probability of class Y given features X.

$P(X|Y)$ is the likelihood of features given class Y.

$P(Y)$ is the prior probability of class Y.

$P(X)$ is the evidence or marginal likelihood of the features. ### 1.3 Types of Naive Bayes Classifiers

There are three primary types of Naive Bayes classifiers:

Gaussian Naive Bayes: Assumes that the features follow a Gaussian (normal) distribution.

Multinomial Naive Bayes: Designed for discrete data, particularly suitable for document classification.

Bernoulli Naive Bayes: Also used for discrete data but works with binary features. ### 1.4 Implementation in R

Let's implement a Naive Bayes classifier using the popular `e1071` package in R:

```R

# Install the package if you haven't already install.packages("e1071")

# Load required libraries library(e1071)
```

```
# Load dataset data(iris) set.seed(123)

# Split the dataset into training and test sets index <- sample(1:nrow(iris), 0.7 * nrow(iris)) train_data <- iris[index, ]

test_data <- iris[-index, ]
# Build the Naive Bayes model

nb_model <- naiveBayes(Species ~ ., data = train_data)

# Make predictions

predictions <- predict(nb_model, test_data)

# Confusion matrix and accuracy

confusion_matrix <- table(test_data$Species, predictions) accuracy <- sum(diag(confusion_matrix)) / sum(confusion_matrix)

print(confusion_matrix)

print(paste("Accuracy:", round(accuracy * 100, 2), "%"))
```
```

### 1.5 Pros and Cons

**Pros**:

Simple and efficient.

Works well with high-dimensional data.

Requires a small amount of training data.

**Cons**:

The independence assumption can lead to poor performance in some cases.

Not suitable for features that are highly correlated.

141
```

Section 2: Ensemble Methods

2.1 Overview of Ensemble Learning

Ensemble methods combine multiple learning algorithms to obtain better predictive performance than could be obtained from any individual model. The underlying philosophy is that "a group of weak learners can form a strong learner."

2.2 Types of Ensemble Methods

Bagging (Bootstrap Aggregating): Reduces variance by training multiple models on different random subsets of the training data and averaging their predictions.

Boosting: Combines weak learners sequentially, where each new learner focuses on the errors made by the previous ones.

Stacking: Combines different types of models (base learners) and uses another model (meta-learner) to make final predictions.

2.3 Implementation in R

R provides several packages for building ensemble models, including `caret`, `randomForest`, and `xgboost`. Below, we implement a Random Forest model using the `randomForest` package:

```R
# Install the package if you haven't already
install.packages("randomForest")

# Load required libraries
library(randomForest)
```

```
# Load dataset (Using the same iris dataset for consistency) set.seed(123)
# Train the Random Forest model
rf_model <- randomForest(Species ~ ., data = train_data, ntree = 100)
# Make predictions
rf_predictions <- predict(rf_model, test_data)
# Confusion matrix and accuracy
rf_confusion_matrix <- table(test_data$Species, rf_predictions)    rf_accuracy <- sum(diag(rf_confusion_matrix)) / sum(rf_confusion_matrix)
print(rf_confusion_matrix)
print(paste("Accuracy:", round(rf_accuracy * 100, 2), "%"))
```
```

### 2.4 Pros and Cons

**Pros**:

Often provides better accuracy than single classifiers.

Robust to overfitting, especially with bagging.

Can handle large datasets effectively.

**Cons**:

More computationally expensive than individual models.

Less interpretable due to the complexity of model combinations. ### 2.5 Boosting with XGBoost
```

XGBoost (Extreme Gradient Boosting) is a popular and efficient implementation of the gradient boosting framework. Here's a brief example:

```R
# Install the package if you haven't already install.packages("xgboost")

# Load required libraries library(xgboost)

# Prepare data in a matrix format

train_matrix <- model.matrix(Species ~ . - 1, data = train_data) test_matrix <- model.matrix(Species ~ . - 1, data = test_data)


# Train Model

xgb_model <- xgboost(data = train_matrix, label = as.numeric(train_data$Species) - 1, nrounds = 100, objective = "multi:softmax", num_class = 3)

# Predictions

xgb_predictions <- predict(xgb_model, test_matrix)

# Confusion matrix and accuracy

xgb_confusion_matrix <- table(test_data$Species, levels(xgb_predictions)) xgb_accuracy <- sum(diag(xgb_confusion_matrix)) / sum(xgb_confusion_matrix)

print(xgb_confusion_matrix)

print(paste("Accuracy:", round(xgb_accuracy * 100, 2), "%"))
```

```
```

Both techniques offer unique advantages and can be used effectively for various classification tasks. As you continue your journey into machine learning, mastering these methods will significantly enhance your data analysis toolkit, allowing you to select the most appropriate approach based on the problem at hand.

Chapter 10: Unsupervised Learning - Clustering Algorithms

In this chapter, we will delve into one of the most popular unsupervised learning techniques: clustering. We will explore various clustering algorithms and implement them in R, a programming language widely used for statistical analysis and data visualization.

10.1 Introduction to Clustering

Clustering is a method of grouping a set of objects in such a way that objects in the same group, known as clusters, are more similar to each other than to those in other groups. It is primarily used for exploratory data analysis, finding natural groupings in data, and reducing the dimensionality of datasets. Clustering can be applied across various domains, including market segmentation, social network analysis, organization of computing clusters, and image compression.

10.2 Types of Clustering Techniques

There are several types of clustering algorithms, each with its advantages and applications. The main categories include:

10.2.1 Partitioning Methods

These methods involve dividing the dataset into distinct clusters, with each element belonging to one cluster. The most well-known algorithm in this category is K-means clustering.

10.2.2 Hierarchical Methods

Hierarchical clustering algorithms create a tree-like

structure (dendrogram) to represent the nested grouping of data. These can be agglomerative (merging) or divisive (splitting).

10.2.3 Density-Based Methods

Density-based clustering detects clusters based on the density of data points in the area. The most notable algorithm is DBSCAN (Density-Based Spatial Clustering of Applications with Noise).

10.2.4 Model-Based Methods

These methods assume that the data is generated by a mixture of underlying probability distributions. Gaussian Mixture Models (GMM) are a prime example of model-based clustering.

10.3 The K-means Clustering Algorithm

K-means is one of the simplest and most efficient clustering methods. It partitions the dataset into K clusters, where K is defined beforehand. The algorithm follows these steps:

Initialization: Randomly select K centroids (cluster centers) from the data.

Assignment: Assign each data point to the nearest centroid, forming K clusters.

Update: Recalculate the centroids as the mean of all points assigned to each cluster.

Convergence: Repeat steps 2 and 3 until the centroids no longer move significantly or maximum iterations are reached.

Implementing K-means in R

To illustrate K-means clustering, let's work with the famous Iris dataset, which contains measurements for three species of iris flowers.

```R
# Load necessary libraries library(ggplot2)

# Load the iris dataset data(iris)

# View the first few rows of the dataset head(iris)

# Remove the species column for clustering iris_data <- iris[, -5]

# Set seed for reproducibility set.seed(123)

# Perform K-means clustering with K=3
kmeans_result <- kmeans(iris_data, centers = 3, nstart = 25)

# Check the clustering result kmeans_result$cluster

# Visualize the clusters
iris$Cluster <- as.factor(kmeans_result$cluster)

ggplot(iris, aes(x = Sepal.Length, y = Sepal.Width, color = Cluster)) + geom_point() +

labs(title = "K-means Clustering of Iris Data") + theme_minimal()
```

This code implements K-means clustering, assigns clusters to the data, and visualizes the results. ## 10.4 Hierarchical Clustering

Hierarchical clustering creates a tree structure to

represent the data. It can be performed using two approaches: agglomerative (bottom-up) and divisive (top-down). We will focus on agglomerative clustering.

Implementing Hierarchical Clustering in R

Let's use the same Iris dataset to demonstrate hierarchical clustering.

```R
# Compute the distance matrix for the iris data
dist_matrix <- dist(iris_data)
# Perform hierarchical clustering
hclust_result <- hclust(dist_matrix, method = "ward.D2")
# Plot the dendrogram plot(hclust_result, labels = iris$Species)


# Cut the dendrogram to create 3 clusters clusters <- cutree(hclust_result, k = 3) iris$HC_Cluster <- as.factor(clusters)
# Visualize the clusters
ggplot(iris, aes(x = Sepal.Length, y = Sepal.Width, color = HC_Cluster)) + geom_point() +
labs(title = "Hierarchical Clustering of Iris Data") + theme_minimal()
```

In this example, we compute the distance matrix, perform hierarchical clustering, and then visualize the resulting clusters.

10.5 Density-Based Clustering - DBSCAN

DBSCAN identifies clusters based on density and can find arbitrarily shaped clusters. It is robust to noise and outliers, making it suitable for real-world datasets that may contain inconsistencies.

Implementing DBSCAN in R

We will use the `dbscan` package to apply DBSCAN on a synthetic dataset.

```R
# Load necessary library library(dbscan)

# Create synthetic data set.seed(456)

data <- rbind(matrix(rnorm(200, mean = 0), ncol = 2),
matrix(rnorm(200, mean = 3), ncol = 2))

# Apply DBSCAN

dbscan_result <- dbscan(data, eps = 0.5, minPts = 5)

# Visualize the clusters

plot(dbscan_result, data = data, main = "DBSCAN Clustering")
```

In this section, we created synthetic data and applied the DBSCAN algorithm to identify clusters. ## 10.6 Model-Based Clustering - Gaussian Mixture Models (GMM)

GMM is a probabilistic model that assumes data is generated from a mixture of several Gaussian distributions. It is particularly useful for identifying clusters when data distribution is complex.

Implementing GMM in R

We'll use the `mclust` package to perform Gaussian Mixture Modeling.

```R
# Load necessary library library(mclust)


# Fit a Gaussian Mixture Model gmm_result <- Mclust(iris_data)

# Summary of the model summary(gmm_result)

# Visualize the GMM clusters plot(gmm_result, what = "classification")
```

This code fits a Gaussian Mixture Model to the Iris dataset and visualizes the resulting clusters.

We learned about the fundamental concepts of unsupervised learning and clustering algorithms. We explored K-means, hierarchical clustering, density-based clustering (DBSCAN), and model-based clustering (GMM) with R. Each method has its strengths and weaknesses, and the choice of algorithm depends on the specific characteristics of the dataset and the analysis goals.

k-Means and Hierarchical Clustering

This chapter will explore both techniques, providing practical examples using R programming. ## 1. Introduction to Clustering

Clustering is a type of unsupervised learning where the goal is to group a set of objects in such a way that objects in the same group (or cluster) are more similar to each other than to those in other groups. This is particularly useful for exploratory data analysis, pattern recognition, and image segmentation.

1.1 Importance of Clustering

Data Reduction: Clustering reduces large datasets into smaller, more manageable groups while preserving essential characteristics.

Anomaly Detection: Identifying outliers can be achieved by examining which groups data points do not belong to.

Market Segmentation: Businesses can identify distinct consumer segments based on purchasing patterns.

Social Network Analysis: Clustering can reveal communities or influential individuals within a network.

2. k-Means Clustering

2.1 Overview of k-Means

k-means clustering assigns data points to one of k clusters based on similarity, measured by Euclidean distance. The algorithm works as follows:

Initialize k centroids randomly.

Assign each data point to the nearest centroid.

Update the centroid of each cluster by calculating the mean of all points assigned to it.

Repeat steps 2 and 3 until the centroids no longer change significantly. ### 2.2 Implementation of k-Means in R

To illustrate k-means clustering in R, we will use the built-in `iris` dataset.

```R
# Load necessary libraries library(ggplot2)
# Load the iris dataset data(iris)
head(iris)
# Select only the numerical columns for clustering
iris_data <- iris[, -5]
# Set a seed for reproducibility set.seed(42)
# Apply k-means clustering with k=3 kmeans_result <-
kmeans(iris_data, centers=3)
# Add cluster information to the original dataset
iris$Cluster <- as.factor(kmeans_result$cluster)
# Visualize the results
ggplot(iris, aes(x = Sepal.Length, y = Sepal.Width, color =
Cluster)) + geom_point(size = 3) +
labs(title = "k-Means Clustering of Iris Dataset") +
theme_minimal()
```

2.3 Choosing the Right k

The choice of k is crucial for k-means clustering. A common approach is the **Elbow Method**:

Run k-means for a range of k values.

Calculate the total within-cluster sum of squares (WSS) for each k.

Plot k against the WSS and look for an "elbow" point

153

where the decrease in WSS starts to taper off.

```R

# Calculate total WSS for different values of k wss <- numeric(10)

for (i in 1:10) {

kmeans_model <- kmeans(iris_data, centers = i) wss[i] <- kmeans_model$tot.withinss

}

# Plot the Elbow Method

plot(1:10, wss, type = "b", pch = 19, xlab = "Number of clusters (k)", ylab = "Total within-cluster sum of squares")
```

3. Hierarchical Clustering

3.1 Overview of Hierarchical Clustering

Hierarchical clustering builds a hierarchy of clusters through either agglomerative (bottom-up) or divisive (top-down) methods. The agglomerative approach is more common and typically follows these steps:

Treat each data point as an individual cluster.

Merge the two closest clusters to form a new cluster.

Repeat until only one cluster remains or a specified number of clusters is reached. ### 3.2 Implementation of Hierarchical Clustering in R

We will demonstrate hierarchical clustering using the same `iris` dataset.

```R
```

```R
# Compute the distance matrix distance_matrix <-
dist(iris_data)

# Perform hierarchical clustering using complete linkage
hc_result    <-    hclust(distance_matrix,    method    =
"complete")

# Visualize the dendrogram

plot(hc_result, labels = iris$Species, main = "Hierarchical
Clustering Dendrogram")
```

3.3 Cutting the Dendrogram

To create a specific number of clusters from the
hierarchical clustering result, you can "cut" the
dendrogram.

```R
# Cut the dendrogram into 3 clusters clusters <-
cutree(hc_result, k = 3)

# Add cluster information to the original dataset
iris$Cluster_HC <- as.factor(clusters)

# Visualize the results

ggplot(iris, aes(x = Sepal.Length, y = Sepal.Width, color =
Cluster_HC)) + geom_point(size = 3) +

labs(title = "Hierarchical Clustering of Iris Dataset") +
theme_minimal()
```

4. Comparison of k-Means and Hierarchical Clustering
4.1 Key Differences

Algorithm Type: k-means is a partitional clustering method, while hierarchical clustering builds a tree structure.

Scalability: k-means is generally faster and more suitable for larger datasets. Hierarchical clustering can be computationally intensive, especially for larger datasets.

Shape of Clusters: k-means assumes spherical clusters, while hierarchical methods can capture a more complex shape.

4.2 When to Use Which?

Use **k-means** when you have a large dataset with a predefined number of clusters, and when the clusters are roughly spherical.

Use **hierarchical clustering** when you want to explore the data without a predefined number of clusters and when you are interested in the hierarchy of the data.

Understanding how to implement these methods effectively in R can significantly enhance one's data analysis capabilities. As you experiment with clustering techniques, remember to explore your dataset thoroughly, choose appropriate parameters, and visualize your results to draw meaningful insights.

Visualizing and Interpreting Cluster Results

Once you have completed the clustering process, the next critical step is to visualize and interpret the results effectively. Visual representations can significantly enhance our understanding of the underlying data structure and the characteristics of each cluster. In this chapter, we will explore various methods and techniques to visualize and interpret clustering results using R programming.

1. Understanding Clustering Results

Before diving into visualizations, it's important to understand the types of clustering algorithms commonly used in R, such as K-means, hierarchical clustering, and DBSCAN. Each algorithm has its own strengths and weaknesses, and they can produce different results on the same dataset. Therefore, it is crucial to interpret the results in the context of your specific problem and data characteristics.

1.1 Evaluating Clusters

Once you have performed clustering, you can evaluate the effectiveness of your clusters using metrics like silhouette width, the elbow method, and within-cluster sum of squares. Understanding these metrics facilitates better interpretation of the clusters:

Silhouette Width: Measures how similar an object is to its own cluster compared to other clusters. A higher silhouette width indicates better-defined clusters.

Elbow Method: A graphical method used to determine the optimal number of clusters by examining the point at which adding more clusters does not lead to an increase in explained variance.

Within-cluster Sum of Squares (WCSS): Measures the variability of the points within each cluster. Lower WCSS values indicate tighter clustering.

2. Visualizing Clusters

Visualization is pivotal in clustering analysis, as it allows us to see the distribution of data points and the boundaries between clusters. Below, we explore several popular visualization techniques available in R.

2.1 Scatter Plot

A scatter plot is one of the simplest ways to visualize clusters, especially in two-dimensional space. The

`ggplot2` library provides an elegant approach to producing scatter plots.

```R
```R library(ggplot2) library(cluster)

# Assuming 'data' is your dataset, and 'clusters' is the vector of cluster assignments data$cluster <- factor(clusters)

ggplot(data, aes(x = feature1, y = feature2, color = cluster)) + geom_point(size = 3) +

labs(title = "Scatter Plot of Clustering Results", x = "Feature 1",

y = "Feature 2") +

theme_minimal()
```
```

2.2 Pair Plot

For datasets with more than two dimensions, a pair plot can help visualize the relationships between multiple features and their associated clusters.

```R
```R library(GGally)
```
```

```
ggpairs(data, aes(color = cluster)) +
```

labs(title = "Pair Plot of Clustering Results") + theme_minimal()
```
```

2.3 Silhouette Plot

A silhouette plot can provide insights into the clustering structure and how well-separated the clusters are. The `cluster` library in R can be used for this purpose.

```R
library(cluster)
```

sil <- silhouette(clusters, dist(data)) plot(sil, main = "Silhouette Plot")
```
```

2.4 Dendrogram

For hierarchical clustering, dendrograms provide a visual representation of the cluster hierarchy.

```R
```

hc <- hclust(dist(data), method = "ward.D2") plot(hc, main = "Dendrogram of Clustering")
```
```

3. Interpreting the Results

Interpreting the results involves more than merely examining the visualizations. It requires a comprehensive understanding of the clusters, including their characteristics and how they relate to the original data.

3.1 Descriptive Statistics

Calculating descriptive statistics for each cluster can give you insights into the key features that define them.

```R
library(dplyr)
cluster_summary <- data %>% group_by(cluster) %>%
summarise_all(list(mean = mean, median = median, sd = sd), na.rm = TRUE)
print(cluster_summary)
```

3.2 Comparison of Clusters

To interpret clusters meaningfully, you may want to compare them using boxplots or violin plots for critical features:

```R
ggplot(data, aes(x = cluster, y = feature1)) + geom_boxplot() +
labs(title = "Comparison of Feature 1 Across Clusters") + theme_minimal()
```

Finally, to make the clustering results actionable, contextualize clusters based on domain knowledge. Understanding what each cluster represents in the real world will guide further analysis or decision-making.

Visualizing and interpreting clustering results is a fundamental step in data analysis and machine learning. Proper visualization can reveal patterns that might not be immediately apparent from raw numerical data alone.

Conclusion

In conclusion, R programming has proven to be an invaluable tool in the realm of machine learning and predictive modeling. Throughout this eBook, we've journeyed from the foundational concepts of R to the intricacies of building, assessing, and deploying machine learning models. As we wrap up, let's reflect on key takeaways and next steps.

We began by understanding the basics of R and its unique capabilities for statistical analysis and data visualization. R's rich ecosystem, with its diverse set of packages and libraries, offers unparalleled flexibility for tackling various predictive modeling challenges. You have learned how to preprocess data effectively, ensuring that your models are trained on quality datasets, which is crucial for achieving accurate predictions.

We also explored different machine learning algorithms, ranging from linear regression to complex ensemble methods. You've seen how to apply these techniques to real-world data, gaining insights into their strengths and weaknesses. By engaging with hands-on examples and case studies, you've developed a practical understanding of how to leverage R for tasks such as classification, regression, and clustering.

Evaluating model performance was another vital component of our journey. We discussed various metrics and validation techniques, empowering you to assess the effectiveness of your models critically. This knowledge is essential not only for selecting the best model but also for communicating results confidently and effectively to stakeholders.

As you move forward, we encourage you to keep exploring the wealth of resources available within the R community. Engaging with forums, attending workshops, and staying updated on the latest packages will further enhance your skills. Remember that practice is key—aim to tackle diverse datasets and projects to solidify your understanding and adaptability in real-world scenarios.

In closing, R programming provides a robust framework for building predictive models that can drive decision-making across industries. Whether you are a data scientist, researcher, or enthusiast, the ability to harness machine learning with R will open doors to innovative solutions and insights. Embrace the journey ahead, continue to learn and experiment, and enjoy the power of predictive modeling that R can offer.

Thank you for joining us on this exploration of R programming for machine learning. We wish you success in your future endeavors and hope that you continue to unlock the potential of data-driven insights. Happy coding!

Biography

Peter Simon is a passionate explorer of patterns, possibilities, and the profound power of data. With a deep-rooted love for *Simon*—the very subject of this eBook—Peter brings a unique blend of technical expertise and creative insight to his writing. His journey began in the world of numbers and logic, where he discovered that behind every dataset lies a story waiting to be told.

Armed with a background in data science and a mastery of tools like R programming and machine learning, Peter has spent years diving into the intricacies of data analysis to uncover meaning, drive innovation, and solve real-world problems. Whether he's building predictive models or visualizing complex insights, his work is guided by curiosity and a desire to make knowledge accessible and impactful.

When he's not immersed in code or statistical models, Peter enjoys exploring the crossroads of technology and creativity. He finds inspiration in teaching others, mentoring aspiring data scientists, and contributing to open-source projects that push the boundaries of what's possible.

This eBook is a reflection of Peter's passion—for Simon, for science, and for the transformative power of understanding. His goal is simple: to empower you with the tools and insights to explore new horizons, just as he has.

Glossary: R Programming for Machine Learning

A

Algorithm: A step-by-step procedure or formula for solving a problem. In the context of machine learning, algorithms process data and create models that can predict outcomes.

Artificial Intelligence (AI)**: A broader field encompassing techniques that allow machines to simulate human intelligence, including machine learning and deep learning.

--- ### B

Bagging (Bootstrap Aggregating)**: An ensemble method that generates multiple versions of a predictive model and combines them to improve accuracy and reduce variance.

--- ### C

Classification**: A supervised learning task that involves predicting categorical labels based on input features. Common algorithms for classification include logistic regression, decision trees, and support vector machines.

Cross-Validation**: A statistical method used to estimate the skill of machine learning models. It involves partitioning the data into subsets and using them to train and test the model iteratively.

--- ### D

Data Frame**: A two-dimensional, table-like structure in R that holds data. It is a key data type in R for organizing data before analysis.

Deep Learning**: A subset of machine learning that utilizes neural networks with multiple layers (deep architectures) to model complex patterns in large datasets.

--- ### E

Ensemble Learning**: Techniques that combine

multiple models to produce better predictions than any single model. Common methods include bagging, boosting, and stacking.

--- ### F

Feature Engineering: The process of selecting, modifying, or creating new features from raw data to improve model performance.

Feature Selection: The process of identifying and selecting a subset of relevant features for use in model construction. This helps to reduce overfitting and improve model interpretability.

--- ### G

Gradient Descent: An optimization algorithm used to minimize the error function in machine learning models by iteratively adjusting model parameters.

--- ### H

Hyperparameter: A parameter whose value is set before the learning process begins. Hyperparameters define the model architecture and training process, and tuning them can significantly affect model performance.

--- ### I

Imputation: The process of filling in missing values in a dataset. This can be done using various techniques, like mean substitution or more complex algorithms.

Input Features: The attributes or independent variables used by machine learning models to make predictions.

--- ### J

Joint Distribution: A statistical distribution representing the probability of two or more variables occurring simultaneously. Understanding joint distributions is crucial for multivariate analysis.

--- ### K

K-means Clustering: A popular unsupervised learning algorithm that partitions a dataset into K distinct clusters based on distance metrics.

--- ### L

Learning Rate: A hyperparameter that determines the step size at each iteration when optimizing a model. It controls how quickly a model learns during training.

--- ### M

Model Evaluation: The process of assessing the performance of a machine learning model using various metrics (such as accuracy, precision, recall, F1-score) and validation techniques (like cross- validation and test datasets).

Normalization: The process of scaling data to fall within a specific range, typically [0, 1] or [-1, 1], which can improve the performance of machine learning algorithms.

--- ### N

Neural Network: A computational model inspired by the human brain, consisting of interconnected nodes (neurons) that can learn complex patterns in data.

--- ### O

Overfitting: A modeling error that occurs when a model captures noise in the training data instead of the underlying data distribution. This leads to poor performance on unseen data.

--- ### P

Predictive Modeling: The process of creating a model that can make predictions about future outcomes based on historical data.

Principal Component Analysis (PCA): A dimensionality reduction technique that transforms high-dimensional data into a lower-dimensional space while preserving variance, often used for exploratory data analysis.

--- ### Q

Quality Metrics: Various statistical measures used to evaluate the quality of a machine learning model, including accuracy, precision, recall, and area under the ROC curve (AUC).

--- ### R

R Language: A programming language and software environment for statistical computing and graphics, widely used in data analysis and machine learning.

Random Forest: An ensemble learning method that builds multiple decision trees and merges them to obtain a more accurate and stable prediction. It's particularly effective for classification and regression tasks.

--- ### S

Supervised Learning: A type of machine learning where the model is trained on labeled data. The objective is to learn a mapping from input features to output labels.

Support Vector Machine (SVM): A supervised machine learning algorithm used for classification and regression tasks, particularly effective in high-dimensional spaces.

T

Training Set: A subset of the dataset used to train a machine learning model. The model learns the underlying patterns from this data.

Test Set: A separate subset of the dataset used to evaluate the performance of a trained model. It provides a measure of how well the model generalizes to unseen data.

--- ### U

Unsupervised Learning: A type of machine learning where the model is trained on data without labeled responses. The main goal is to find hidden patterns or intrinsic structures in the data.

--- ### V

Validation Set: An independent subset of the dataset used to fine-tune model parameters and avoid overfitting before testing on the final test set.

--- ### W

Weight: Parameters in a machine learning model that are adjusted during training to minimize prediction error. Weights determine the influence of input features on the output prediction.

www.ingramcontent.com/pod-product-compliance
Lightning Source LLC
La Vergne TN
LVHW052059060326
832903LV00061B/3629